Poems Under Saturn / Poèmes saturniens

C000163386

THE LOCKERT LIBRARY OF POETRY IN TRANSLATION

Editorial advisor: Richard Howard

For other titles in the Lockert Library, see p. 153

Poems Under Saturn / Poèmes saturniens

Paul Verlaine

TRANSLATED AND WITH
AN INTRODUCTION BY
Karl Kirchwey

PRINCETON UNIVERSITY PRESS   *Princeton and Oxford*

Copyright 2011 © by Princeton University Press
Published by Princeton University Press, 41 William Street,
Princeton, New Jersey 08540
In the United Kingdom: Princeton University Press, 6 Oxford Street,
Woodstock, Oxfordshire OX20 1TW
press.princeton.edu

Jacket art: Léon Frédéric, *L'intérieur d'atelier* (detail). © Collection Musée d'Ixelles, Brussels. Photo by Mixed Media.

Library of Congress Cataloging-in-Publication Data
Verlaine, Paul, 1844–1896
  [Poèmes saturniens. English]
  Poems under Saturn = Poèmes saturniens / Paul Verlaine ; translated
[from the French] by Karl Kirchwey.
      p. cm. — (The Lockert Library of poetry in translation)
   ISBN 978-0-691-14485-6 (cloth: alk. paper) — ISBN 978-0-691-14486-3
(pbk. : alk.paper) 1. Verlaine, Paul, 1844–1896—Translations into English.
I. Kirchwey, Karl, 1956– II. Title.
  PQ2463.P5713 2011
  841'.8–dc22   2010016440

British Library Cataloging-in-Publication Data is available

The Lockert Library of Poetry in Translation is supported
by a bequest from Charles Lacy Lockert (1888–1974)

This book has been composed in Garamond Premier
Designed and composed by Tracy Baldwin
Printed on acid-free paper. ∞
Printed in the United States of America

10 9 8 7 6 5 4 3 2 1

Contents

Acknowledgments

The French text (included here *en face*) is that provided by Project Gutenberg and has been cross-checked against the Bibliothèque de la Pléiade edition *Verlaine: Oeuvres poétiques complètes* (1962). The introduction and critical notes assembled by Martine Bercot in the Livre de Poche edition of the *Poèmes saturniens* (1996) are invaluable and a model of textual scholarship. I have relied on her notes frequently in my own, and have acknowledged them. The notes by Le Dantec and Borel in the Pléiade edition are also helpful.

I would like to thank Christine Couffin, Michèle Champagnat, Cathérine Dana, and Bryn Mawr College Professor of French (Emeritus) Mario Maurin for their help with this translation. Hanne Winarsky, Literature Editor of Princeton University Press, was loyal to this project even in its earliest (and roughest) stages.

"Parisian Sketch," "Nightmare," "Jesuitism," and "The Song of the Ingénues," together with the Introduction, appeared (in earlier versions) in the Spring 2008 issue of *Parnassus: Poetry in Review*, and I would also like to thank Herbert Leibowitz and Ben Downing for their encouragement. "Resignation," "After Three Years," "Night Effect," "Sentimental Stroll," "Mister Wiseman," "Serenade," and "Marco" appeared in the inaugural issue of *Little Star* (Spring 2011), and thanks are due to Ann Kjellberg, editor of that journal, for her interest.

This translation is dedicated to the memory of Colette Brèque.

Introduction

In the late summer of 2006, I began to translate a few favorite early Verlaine poems. This innocent amusement somehow became an obsession—and a kind of love affair. What has by now become a complete translation of Verlaine's first book, the *Poèmes saturniens (Poems Under Saturn)* of 1866—so far as I know the only complete translation of the book in English—began with two motivations common to most, if not all, translations: admiration for the original work, and a certain impatience with the existing translations. Of the former I shall say more in a moment.

The Verlaine translations I knew first were those by C. F. MacIntyre (dating from 1948), which have long been standard in English. Yet I came to feel that these somehow condescend, both to Verlaine and to the contemporary reader, in a way that simply would not do. They also ride on now-unaccountable complacencies of culture and gender, even after we make allowances for those present in the original. "How fresh and adolescent the whole poem is!" MacIntyre exclaims at one point; elsewhere, he speaks of "Those lovely girls of one's first fine flush of rapture!" Often, in his attempt to preserve Verlaine's rhymes, MacIntyre sacrifices syntax or diction or both, and includes padding, as do later translations of Verlaine by Doris-Jeanne Gourévitch (1970).

Joanna Richardson's translations (1974) alternate between free verse and metrical verse, though meter shapes some of her best lines. Her commitment to rhyme is similarly variable. Among contemporary translations, Norman Shapiro's (1999) are probably the most successful, but like the other translators mentioned so far, he is trying to represent the whole span of Verlaine's work in a single volume.

Martin Sorrell's translations in the Oxford World's Classics series also date from 1999. These are, however, unrhymed, and indeed, the translator declares that "the worst tyranny for any translator of Verlaine was rhyme" (p. xxx) By taking it for granted that rhyme "does not anyway have such a strong place in modern English prosody," Sorrell clears the way for his own free verse translations. But in fact rhyme is alive and well in both contemporary English and American poetry, and ignoring it in the hopes of sounding more "contemporary" seems too easy. Furthermore, in a "critique" of the *Poèmes saturniens* he wrote in 1890 at the time of the reissue of his first book, Verlaine speaks of those who would accuse him of "timidity" with regard to *vers libre*, and retorts, "My God, I thought I had smashed verse enough, I thought I had freed it enough, if you like, in displacing the caesura as much as possible, and with regard to rhyme, making use of it with discretion, though, without constraining myself much to employ either pure assonances or inconsiderately excessive types of echo." ("Mon Dieu, j'ai cru avoir assez brisé le vers, l'avoir assez affranchi, si vous préférez, en déplaçant la césure le plus possible, et quant à la rime, m'en être servi avec quelque judiciaire pourtant, en ne m'astreignant pas trop, soit à de pures assonances, soit à des formes de l'écho indiscrètement excessives." Le Dantec/Borel, 1074.) From this point of view, the use of rhyme is an actual imperative if the translator is to remain faithful to Verlaine's original and to its innovation.

I felt, therefore, that there was room for a fresh attempt, and one that would restore some of these often-anthologized poems to their original context in Verlaine's first book. Robert Bly has remarked that "the best translation resembles a Persian rug seen from the back—the pattern is apparent, but not much more" (Bly, 48). In thinking about what part of Verlaine's "pattern" to concentrate on first, I was guided by my own practice of thirty years in writing and publishing poems in English, and decided that I would preserve, poem by poem, Verlaine's diverse schemes of end-rhyme. Bly further opines that "I believe in working as much as possible with internal rhymes, but I think it's best not to insist on reproducing end rhymes . . . .the translator has to add images that destroy the poem's integrity" (Bly, 44). However, I resolved that I would seek to avoid both such padding of images and the earlier translators' compromises of syntax, while trying to preserve an English language diction infused with as much as possible of the range of the French original, which as I understand it mines high and low, academic and colloquial. As Paul Valéry remarks of Verlaine, "His verse, free and moving between the extremes of language, dares stoop from the most delicately musical tone to prose, sometimes to the basest of prose, which he borrows and adopts deliberately" ("Son vers, libre et mobile entre les extrêmes du langage, ose descendre du ton le plus délicatement musical jusqu'à la prose, parfois à la pire des proses, qu'il emprunte et qu'il épouse délibérément"; Valéry, 183). There is a striking lexical energy in this book, and, without being seduced by false cognates, the translator must rejoice at the opportunity to carry into English words like "bister" ("bistre"), "amaranth" ("amarante"), or "wyvern" ("guivre"). In any case, the translator who obeys Bly's judgment about end-rhyme, in the case of Verlaine (or of Rilke, who was Bly's subject) is depriving the reader of one of the chief auditory beauties of the original poetry.

In order to maintain as close a fidelity to Verlaine's original as possible, I have defined "rhyme" in English with a latitude that is conscious of work by American poets such as Robert Pinsky in his 1994 translation *The Inferno of Dante*. Pinsky proved the viability of rhyme over the long haul with the notoriously restrictive form of terza rima. In his "Translator's Note" to that volume, Pinsky describes pitfalls of the kind that presumably made Bly give up on end-rhyme: "squeezing unlikely synonyms to the ends of lines, and bending idiom ruthlessly to get them there" (Pinsky, xix). In order to avoid these, seeking what he calls an "audible scaffold," Pinsky widens the spectrum of rhyme so that it includes "the same consonant-sounds—however much vowels may differ—at the ends of words" (Pinsky, xix). My translation has relied upon a system of rhyme that ranges from perfect (masculine rhymes like "yell" and "swell," "leaps" and "weeps"; feminine rhymes such as "plastic" and "fantastic") through a spectrum of imperfect rhyme, from consonant rhyme ("citrus" and "boleros," "coast" and "rest") through more approximate rhymes, such as "waves" and "wreathes," "flesh" and "Electra," "zigzags" and "masks," "ingénues" and "known," and "ecstatic" and "Viaticum." Throughout, the change from singular to plural is forgiven, as part of the rhyme: "reeds" and "onward," "swans" and "green," "fast" and "artists," etcetera.

To be sure, there are sound effects in Verlaine's first book that cannot be rendered in English, such as the complex crossed internal rhymes of lines like "Des bouts de fumée en forme de cinq / Sortaient drus et noirs des hauts toits pointus" ("Shaped like a five, the wisps of smoke / Poured thick and black from the high gables"). An acoustic pun is also lost in translation, such as that in play in the two lines "Comme l'aile d'une orfraie / Qu'un subit orage effraie" ("Like the wing of an osprey / Frightened by the storm's sudden fury"), in which one bird, the osprey or white-tailed eagle ("orfraie"), mingles with another, the barn owl ("effraie"), whose name in French corresponds to a form of the verb "to frighten." Then there is the opening line in "Monsieur Prudhomme," in which the subject is mayor of his town and both mother and father of his family, in French, but only mayor and father, in English ("il est maire et père de famille").

What have been sacrificed, in my version, are Verlaine's syllabic meters, which, as Sorrell points out (Sorrell, xix), both engage with traditional prosody and challenge it. But if it is possible to distinguish between meter and rhythm, I have certainly tried to be sensitive to those exquisite rhythms, in certain of Verlaine's early poems, in which his unique combination of verbal music and psychological state announces itself. This is what Jacques Borel describes, in his Introduction to the Pléiade edition, as "the musical quality of this art ... the magic of a song inseparable from tactile or visual sensations, auditory or olfactory, finally confounded, integrated into the melody through which they are made known to us" ("la qualité musicale de cet art ... la magie d'un chant indissociable des sensations tactiles ou visuelles, auditives ou olfactives finalement fondues, intégrées à la mélodie à laquelle elles se communiquent à nous"; Le Dantec/Borel, 55).

Robert Pinsky has also remarked that "Translation is the highest form of reading." Implicit in what he says, it seems to me, is a notion of translation as a kind of homage to an original, and as an act of absolute attention and comprehension. It might well be asked: why translate Verlaine's first book? Being his first (absent a Rimbaldian precocity), it could hardly be expected to be his best, revealing instead a number of apprentice debts. And the critical consensus is that Verlaine wrote *too much* poetry: that it is always necessary to pick and choose among his poems. As a contemporary American poet, rather than a trained scholar of French, I am less able to offer scholarly or critical justifications for this translation than I am able to reexamine my own initial enthusiasm and admiration.

In the Introduction to his 2000 translation of *Beowulf*, Seamus Heaney speaks of the attraction of translating, of falling in love with the source text: "The erotics of composition are essential to the process, some pre-reflective excitation and orientation, some sense that your own little verse-craft can dock safe and sound at the big quay of the language. And this is as true for translators as it is for poets attempting original work" (Heaney, xxvi). This is what translator Christopher Middleton has described as the translator's feeling that "he might be reweaving the original spell" (Warren, 24). I would take this further and suggest that the profound excitement one experiences in deciding to translate the work of a poet writing in a different language is something like that of discovering a world with which, though it was hitherto unknown, one feels instantly familiar: or of encountering a mind, a sensibility, with which one feels an immediate affinity. In an essay entitled "The Added Artificer," scholar Renato Poggioli describes it this way: "Through the shock of a recognition primarily psychic in quality, the translator suddenly finds that a poem newly discovered, or discovered anew, offers him an exemplary solution for his own formal problems, as well as an expressive outlet for his subjective *Erlebnis* . . . .translation is, both formally and psychologically, a process of inscape, rather than of escape" (Brower, 141–42). And Bly speaks of a stage of translation at which "the translator should ask himself whether the feelings as well as the concepts are within his world. If they are not, he should stop" (Bly, 21).

There is no doubt a risk that such a sense of familiarity will invite the translator to take too much for granted. When a writer finds a kindred spirit in literature, he may assume, like a lover, that he perfectly understands that spirit, whereas true understanding comes with long cohabitation. And there is a different risk of familiarity, too, which is that the translator will simply use the original as a kind of palimpsest upon which to inscribe his own obsessions. Thus Heaney, in describing the process of his translation of the Irish poem he calls *Sweeney Astray* (1983), writes, "[Robert] Lowell's example was operative here. His trick of heightening the sense by adding voltage to the diction and planting new metaphors into the circuit was not lost on me. Nor was his unabashed readiness to subdue the otherness of the original to his own autobiographical neediness. . . . I cuffed the original with a brusqueness and familiarity that was not earned but that gave me immense satisfaction. I was using *Buile Suibhne* as a trampoline . . ." (Warren, 17–18). As Rosanna Warren points out in the Introduction to the anthology in which Heaney's "Notes on Translating *Buile Suibhne*" appear, "We grow by welcoming difference, not by assimilating it entirely to ourselves" (Warren, 5).

The risks of such subjectivity make it seem imperative to find other reasons after all, more external or objective reasons, for translating. So, to speak once again of my admiration for this book of Verlaine's, the first thing that struck me about the *Poèmes saturniens,* along with its range of experience (whether real or imagined), was its erudition. The fact that the young Verlaine is participating in Leconte de Lisle's Parnassian retrospect to the Greeks and the Hindus does not diminish my pleasure in his learning; it is dazzling even if new-minted. As one whose own sense of poetic possibility had been shaped by the Late Modernist intellectual achievements of learned and ambitious poets such as Berryman, Lowell, and Jarrell, I could hardly have responded otherwise.

I also found in Verlaine's first book a confirmation of a notion of poetic originality that is unfashionable at the moment. T. S. Eliot suggested long ago (in his 1917 essay "Tradition and the Individual Talent") that true originality lies in the way the poet responds to what has come before him. And in this first book, Verlaine is deliberately engaging (sometimes down to the phrase and image) with his contemporaries, his predecessors, with the giants of French poetry up to his time. The influence of Baudelaire—all that languor and baleful carnality—is particularly clear. Jacques Borel emphasizes Verlaine's indebtedness to Baudelaire when he says that in this first book, "The break with all earlier poetry, the turning point from which all modern poetry takes its origin, and first of all that of Verlaine himself, could not be more strongly affirmed" ("La cassure avec toute la poésie antérieure, ce tournant majeure à partir duquel toute la poésie moderne prend naissance, et d'abord celle de Verlaine lui-même, ne sauraient être plus résolument affirmés"; Le Dantec/Borel, 50). Furthermore, in an age (our own) in which the aftermath of Confessional poetry has given rise to incomparably tedious vistas of autobiographical verse, there is something invigorating about the Parnassian doctrine of *l'impassible* (the "impassive" or "unmoved"), about the challenge of creating emotion in poetry by means that have little or nothing to do with (traumatic) personal testimonial, with the details of the poet's own experience. And this is true even if the fascination of Verlaine's early poems lies, in part, in the inconsistency of their attitude toward *l'impassible.*

Verlaine's engagement is not just with authors, but with genres of poetry, too. Such is the case with ekphrasis, or poems that speak to works of visual art—fashionable in Verlaine's time as it has become so again in our own. In the same essay, "The School of Giorgione," in which he offers his famous dictum (quite relevant to Verlaine's practice also) that "*All art constantly aspires toward the condition of music,*" Walter Pater remarks upon the analogy "of French poetry generally and the art of engraving." In the section of Verlaine's book called "Eaux-fortes" ("Etchings"), and in particular in a poem like "Effet de nuit" ("Night Effect"), we find lines of poetry that seem to have been carved by some fierce burin with a visual clarity quite equal to the cross-hatched savagery of the image they describe; and the extent to which visual effects contribute to the atmosphere of terror in the later parts of "La mort de Philippe II" ("The Death of Philip II") is uncanny.

I was attracted to these poems not only for their intellect, but for their sensuousness as well, what Norman Shapiro refers to as the "synthesis of the cerebral and the visceral" in Verlaine's work (Shapiro, 3). The intoxications of the flesh, the "smell of bodies young and dear," mingled with self-disgust: the mixture is still a potent one, even after a century and a half. And just as one begins to feel that the worldly irony audible in some of these poems is a kind of late-adolescent posture, a startling and convincing erotic longing erupts in others. This longing has partly to do with Verlaine's rejection of bourgeois values and social pretense. The title of the poem "Jésuitisme" ("Jesuitism"), for example, connotes not just intrigue or equivocation but hypocrisy. And "La chanson des ingénues" ("The Song of the Ingenues") seems to be propelled partly by longing and partly by rage. A recurrent phrase in this book is "sans trèves," that is, "unceasingly, relentlessly," and the drive here (on the part of the twenty-two-year-old author) is to beat down the suffocating confines of mid-nineteenth-century French society.

For Verlaine, not only the intellect and the emotions, but also the spirit, always speak through the body. English author George Moore remarked of Verlaine that "he abandoned himself to the Church as a child to a fairy-tale" (Richardson, *Verlaine*, 133). He is certainly trying on attitudes in these early and secular poems, but there is an energy of feeling that relates them to both the devotional poems of the 1881 volume *Sagesse (Wisdom)* and to the more leering or louche poems of *Chansons pour elle (Songs for Her)*, published in 1891. What one hears in *Poèmes saturniens* is a kind of labile passion that never settles on either the sacred or the profane, the spirit or the body, but instead whipsaws between them, and indeed requires both of them. With good reason, Valéry speaks of "the dark and powerful mixture of mystical emotion and sensual ardor that develop in Verlaine" ("le mélange puissant et trouble de l'émotion mystique et de l'ardeur sensuelle qui se développent dans Verlaine"; Valéry, 173).

In short, much of Verlaine's later work is prefigured by these first poems. In his *Confessions,* written near the end of his life, Verlaine spoke of "these *Poèmes saturniens* in which the self I was then breaks out, strange and a little fierce" ("ces *Poèmes satur-niens* où éclate bien le moi fantasque et quelque peu farouche que j'étais"; Verlaine, 103). Actually, the adjectives Verlaine uses to describe himself, "fantasque" and "farouche," are hard to translate; the first can also mean "fantastical" or "whimsical," and the second can mean "sullen," "unsociable," or "shy." The young Verlaine is all of these things, and in *Poèmes saturniens* he both acknowledges his debts to his elders and explores the extraordinary range of his own voice.

Works Cited

Bly, Robert. *The Eight Stages of Translation*. Boston: Rowan Tree Press, 1983.

Brower, Reuben, ed. *On Translation*. Cambridge: Harvard University Press, 1959.

Heaney, Seamus, trans. *Beowulf: A New Verse Translation*. New York: Farrar, Straus and Giroux, 2000.

Pinsky, Robert, trans. *The "Inferno" of Dante: A New Verse Translation*. New York: Farrar, Straus and Giroux, 1994.

Richardson, Joanna. *Verlaine*. London: Weidenfeld and Nicolson, 1971.

Valéry, Paul. *Variété II*. Paris: Librairie Gallimard (Éditions de la Nouvelle Revue Française), 1930.

Warren, Rosanna, ed. *The Art of Translation: Voices From the Field*. Boston: Northeastern University Press, 1989.

Editions of Works by Verlaine

Bercot, Martine, ed. Verlaine, Paul. *Poèmes saturniens*. Paris: Le Livre de Poche, 1996.

Gaudon, Jean, ed. *Poèmes saturniens et Confessions*. Paris:
    G.F.- Flammarion, 1977.
Gourévitch, Doris-Jeanne, trans. *Paul Verlaine: Selected Verse*.
    Waltham, MA: Blaisdell Publishing Company, 1970.
Le Dantec, Y.-G., and Jacques Borel, eds. *Verlaine: Oeuvres poètiques
    complètes*. Paris: Éditions Gallimard (Bibliothèque de la Pléiade),
    1962.
MacIntyre, C. F., trans. *Paul Verlaine: Selected Poems*. Berkeley:
    University of California Press, 1948.
Richardson, Joanna. *Selected Poems: Verlaine*. New York: Penguin Books,
    1974.
Shapiro, Norman R., trans. *One Hundred and One Poems by Paul
    Verlaine*. Chicago: University of Chicago Press, 1999.
Sorrell, Martin, trans. *Paul Verlaine: Selected Poems*. New York: Oxford
    University Press, 1999.

An ellipses [...] has been used to indicate a stanza break
when poem continues onto a new page.

Poems Under Saturn / Poèmes saturniens

Les Sages d'autrefois, qui valaient bien ceux-ci,
Crurent, et c'est un point encor mal éclairci,
Lire au ciel les bonheurs ainsi que les désastres,
Et que chaque âme était liée à l'un des astres.
(On a beaucoup raillé, sans penser que souvent
Le rire est ridicule autant que décevant,
Cette explication du mystère nocturne.)
Or ceux-là qui sont nés sous le signe SATURNE,
Fauve planète, chère aux nécromanciens,
Ont entre tous, d'après les grimoires anciens,
Bonne part de malheurs et bonne part de bile.
L'Imagination, inquiète et débile,
Vient rendre nul en eux l'effort de la Raison.
Dans leurs veines, le sang, subtil comme un poison,
Brûlant comme une lave, et rare, coule et roule
En grésillant leur triste Idéal qui s'écroule.
Tels les Saturniens doivent souffrir et tels
Mourir,—en admettant que nous soyons mortels,—
Leur plan de vie étant dessiné ligne à ligne
Par la logique d'une Influence maligne.

P. V.

The ancient Sages, like today's worth listening to,
Believed—a point still not elucidated, though—
That in the sky they read both disaster and happiness
And that each soul was bound to one of the stars.
(We scoff a lot at this explanation of
The nightly mystery without thinking that our laugh
Is a ridiculous as well as a disappointing one.)
But those who are born under the sign of SATURN,
Dear to necromancers, tawny planet,
Shared, according to the ancient
Black books, a large part of misfortune and bile.
Imagination, restless and feeble,
In them brings to nothing the effort of Reason.
The blood in their veins flows subtle as a poison,
Burning like lava, rarefied, it rolls,
Crackling their sad Ideal, which crumbles.
So must these Saturnians suffer
And so must die,—admitting that we are
Mortal,—their life's plan sketched out line for line
By the logic of a malignant Sign.

P. V.

Prologue / **Prologue**

Dans ces temps fabuleux, les limbes de l'histoire,
Où les fils de Raghû, beaux de fard et de gloire,
Vers la Ganga régnaient leur règne étincelant,
Et, par l'intensité de leur vertu troublant
Les Dieux et les Démons et Bhagavat lui-même,
Augustes, s'élevaient jusqu'au Néant suprême,
Ah! la terre et la mer et le ciel, purs encor
Et jeunes, qu'arrosait une lumière d'or
Frémissante, entendaient, apaisant leurs murmures
De tonnerres, de flots heurtés, de moissons mûres,
Et retenant le vol obstiné des essaims,
Les Poètes sacrés chanter les Guerriers saints,
Ce pendant que le ciel et la mer et la terre
Voyaient—rouges et las de leur travail austère—
S'incliner, pénitents fauves et timorés,
Les Guerriers saints devant les Poètes sacrés!
Une connexité grandiosement alme
Liait le Kchatrya serein au Chanteur calme,
Valmiki l'excellent à l'excellent Rama:
Telles sur un étang deux touffes de padma.

—Et sous tes cieux dorés et clairs, Hellas antique,
De Spartè la sévère à la rieuse Attique,
Les Aèdes, Orpheus, Alkaïos, étaient
Encore des héros altiers et combattaient,
Homéros, s'il n'a pas, lui, manié le glaive,
Fait retentir, clameur immense qui s'élève,
Vos échos, jamais las, vastes postérités,
D'Hektôr, et d'Odysseus, et d'Akhilleus chantés.

In those fabled eras, the limbo of history
In which the sons of Raghu, handsome with fard and glory,
Extended their brilliant reign toward the Ganga, rivals of
Gods and Demons and Bhagavan himself,
In the intensity of their august virtues,
Ascending toward the supreme Nothingness,
Ah! the earth and the sea and the sky, still pure
And young, sprinkled by a trembling gold shower,
Calming their rumbling thunderheads,
Their ripe harvests and sudden floods,
Restraining their swarms in stubborn flights,
Heard sacred Poets sing of Warrior Saints,
This while the sky and the sea and the earth
Saw—now grown flushed and weary with
Their austere labor—the Warrior Saints bow, chastened,
Their wildness awe-struck, before the sacred Bard!
A close sustaining bond joined them,
Serene Kshatriya and the Singer who was calm,
The excellent Valmiki and the excellent Rama:
As on a pond two clumps of lotus flower.

—And, ancient Hellas, beneath your clear gold sky,
From stern Sparta to laughing Attica,
Orpheus, Alkaïos, the epic poets
Were still lordly heroes and fought in combat.
Homer, if he did not himself wield the sword,
Nonetheless made ring out your unwearied
Echoes, raised immense clamor, great legacies
Sung of Hektor and Odysseus and Akhilleus.

Les héros à leur tour, après les luttes vastes,
Pieux, sacrifiaient aux neuf Déesses chastes,
Et non moins que de l'art d'Arès furent épris
De l'Art dont une Palme immortelle est le prix,
Akhilleus entre tous! Et le Laërtiade
Dompta, parole d'or qui charme et persuade,
Les esprits et les coeurs et les âmes toujours,
Ainsi qu'Orpheus domptait les tigres et les ours.

—Plus tard, vers des climats plus rudes, en des ères
Barbares, chez les Francs tumultueux, nos pères,
Est-ce que le Trouvère héroïque n'eut pas
Comme le Preux sa part auguste des combats?
Est-ce que, Théroldus ayant dit Charlemagne,
Et son neveu Roland resté dans la montagne
Et le bon Olivier et Turpin au grand coeur,
En beaux couplets et sur un rythme âpre et vainqueur,
Est-ce que, cinquante ans après, dans les batailles,
Les durs Leudes perdant leur sang par vingt entailles,
Ne chantaient pas le chant de geste sans rivaux,
De Roland et de ceux qui virent Roncevaux
Et furent de l'énorme et superbe tuerie,
Du temps de l'Empereur à la barbe fleurie? . . .

—Aujourd'hui, l'Action et le Rêve ont brisé
Le pacte primitif par les siècles usé,
Et plusieurs ont trouvé funeste ce divorce
De l'harmonie immense et bleue et de la Force.
La Force qu'autrefois le Poète tenait

The heroes in their turn, after great contests,
Made pious sacrifice to the nine chaste
Muses, and no less than the art of Ares
Loved that Art for which the immortal Palm was the prize,
Akhilleus above all! And Odysseus, Laertes' son,
Tamed the spirit and heart and soul of everyone,
Convinced, enchanted by his golden speech always,
Just as Orpheus tamed the tigers and bears.

—Later, in rougher climates, in barbaric eras,
Among the riotous Franks, our ancestors,
The heroic Trouvère, did he not,
Like the valiant Knight, have his distinguished share of combat?
Did not Theroldus, having sung of Charlemagne
And his nephew Roland who stayed in the mountain
And good Olivier and Turpin the great-hearted
In handsome couplets in which harsh rhythm vaunted,
And, in battles fifty years later,
Did not the hard Liege-Men whose blood would pour
From twenty wounds sing of Roncevaux,
The *Chanson de geste* of Roland and those who saw
And were a part of the huge superb butchery
In the time of the Emperor whose beard was flowery? . . .

—Action and Dream have broken, nowadays,
Their primitive pact worn down by the centuries,
And some have found it disastrous, this divorce
Between immense blue harmony and Force.
Force, that once upon a time the poet bridled,

En bride, blanc cheval ailé qui rayonnait,
La force, maintenant, la Force, c'est la Bête
Féroce bondissante et folle et toujours prête
À tout carnage, à tout dévastement, à tout
Égorgement d'un bout du monde à l'autre bout!
L'Action qu'autrefois réglait le chant des lyres,
Trouble, enivrée, en proie aux cent mille délires
Fuligineux d'un siècle en ébullition,
L'Action à présent,—ô pitié!—l'Action,
C'est l'ouragan, c'est la tempête, c'est la houle
Marine dans la nuit sans étoiles, qui roule
Et déroule parmi des bruits sourds l'effroi vert
Et rouge des éclairs sur le ciel entr'ouvert!

—Cependant, orgueilleux et doux, loin des vacarmes
De la vie et du choc désordonné des armes
Mercenaires, voyez, gravissant les hauteurs
Ineffables, voici le groupe des Chanteurs
Vêtus de blanc, et des lueurs d'apothéoses
Empourprent la fierté sereine de leurs poses:
Tous beaux, tous purs, avec des rayons dans les yeux,
Et sur leur front le rêve inachevé des Dieux!
Le monde, que troublait leur parole profonde,
Les exile. A leur tour ils exilent le monde!
C'est qu'ils ont à la fin compris qu'il ne faut plus
Mêler leur note pure aux cris irrésolus
Que va poussant la foule obscène et violente,
Et que l'isolement sied à leur marche lente.
Le Poète, l'amour du Beau, voilà sa foi,

White-winged steed that dazzled.
Force, now, Force, it is the ferocious
Mad bounding Beast, and always
Ready for any carnage, for any devastation,
From this end of the world to the other one!
Action, once measured by the song of the lyre,
Drunken, disrupts, prey to the hundred thousand obscure
Deliriums of a boiling century,
Action, just now—Action—o pity!—
It is the hurricane, the tempest, the surging tide
In the starless night that will unroll and spread
Amid dull sounds, the red and green terror
Of its lightning bolts through a sky ajar!

—Meanwhile, proud and gentle, far from the uproar
Of life and the undisciplined shock of mercenary war,
See them, ascending the ineffable height,
Here, the group of Singers dressed in white,
And the glimmerings of the setting sun
Reddening the serene pride of their position:
So beautiful, so pure, in their eyes the beam
Of light, in their countenance the Gods' unfinished dream!
Disturbed by their profound speech, the world
Exiles them, and they exile that by which they are exiled!
Because they have finally understood that loneliness suits their
Slow march, that they need no longer mingle their pure
Tone with the crowd's exhalation,
its irresolute cries, violent and obscene.
The Poet, the love of Beauty is his faith, his battle

L'Azur, son étendard, et l'Idéal, sa loi
Ne lui demandez rien de plus, car ses prunelles,
Où le rayonnement des choses éternelles
A mis des visions qu'il suit avidement,
Ne sauraient s'abaisser une heure seulement
Sur le honteux conflit des besognes vulgaires,
Et sur vos vanités plates; et si naguères
On le vit au milieu des hommes, épousant
Leurs querelles, pleurant avec eux, les poussant
Aux guerres, célébrant l'orgueil des Républiques
Et l'éclat militaire et les splendeurs auliques
Sur la kitare, sur la harpe et sur le luth,
S'il honorait parfois le présent d'un salut
Et daignait consentir à ce rôle de prêtre
D'aimer et de bénir, et s'il voulait bien être
La voix qui rit ou pleure alors qu'on pleure ou rit,
S'il inclinait vers l'âme humaine son esprit,
C'est qu'il se méprenait alors sur l'âme humaine.

—Maintenant, va, mon Livre, où le hasard te mène.

Standard the Azure, his law the Ideal!
Ask no more of him, because his eyes,
In which the radiance of eternities
Has put the visions he follows eagerly,
Would not know how to abase themselves even briefly
With the shameful conflict of your low
Tasks, your empty vanities; and if, not long ago,
One saw him amid human beings, taking on their
Quarrels, weeping with them, urging them to war,
Celebrating the pride of their Republics,
Military pomp and the court's bardic
Splendor on the kithara, harp and lute,
If, from time to time, he would honor the present
With a greeting and even deigned to play
The role of priest, to love and bless, and wanted to be
The voice that cried or laughed, when one laughed or cried,
If toward the human soul his spirit bowed,
He was mistaken about the human soul, only that.

—Now go, my Book, where chance may indicate.

Melancholia / **Melancholia**

À Ernest Boutier / *To Ernest Boutier*

I. Résignation

Tout enfant, j'allais rêvant Ko-Hinnor,
Somptuosité persane et papale,
Héliogabale et Sardanapale!

Mon désir créait sous des toits en or,
Parmi les parfums, au son des musiques,
Des harems sans fin, paradis physiques!

Aujourd'hui, plus calme et non moins ardent,
Mais sachant la vie et qu'il faut qu'on plie,
J'ai dû refréner ma belle folie,
Sans me résigner par trop cependant.

Soit! le grandiose échappe à ma dent,
Mais fi de l'aimable et fi de la lie!
Et je hais toujours la femme jolie!
La rime assonante et l'ami prudent.

I. Resignation

When I was little, I went along dreaming of Koh-i-Noor,
A Persian and Papal sumptuousness,
Heliogabalus and Sardanapalus!

Under roofs of worked gold, my desire
Created, amid music and fragrances,
Endless harems, physical paradises!

Nowadays, calmer and no less passionate,
But knowing life and knowing I must bend,
I have been obliged and have restrained
(Though not too much restrained) my lovely fit.

The great slips from my grasp: why then, so be it!
But fie on the pleasant, the no-more-than-gay, and
I hate a routinely pretty woman, a wise friend,
And always and forever a rhyme that is assonant.

II. Nevermore

Souvenir, souvenir, que me veux-tu? L'automne
Faisait voler la grive à travers l'air atone,
Et le soleil dardait un rayon monotone
Sur le bois jaunissant où la bise détone.

Nous étions seul à seule et marchions en rêvant,
Elle et moi, les cheveux et la pensée au vent.
Soudain, tournant vers moi son regard émouvant:
« Quel fut ton plus beau jour! » fit sa voix d'or vivant,

Sa voix douce et sonore, au frais timbre angélique.
Un sourire discret lui donna la réplique,
Et je baisai sa main blanche, dévotement.

—Ah! les premières fleurs, qu'elles sont parfumées!
Et qu'il bruit avec un murmure charmant
Le premier *oui* qui sort de lèvres bien-aimées!

II. Nevermore

Memory, memory, what do you want from me? I remember
Autumn made the thrush fly through the lifeless air,
And the sun launched a monotonous ray where
The north wind exploded in a wood growing yellower.

We were alone together and, dreaming, wandered,
She and I, our hair and our thoughts in the wind.
Suddenly, her gaze full of feeling, she turned:
"What was your happiest day?" Her gold voice, livened,

Her soft resonant voice, cool timbre of an angel.
My reply was a reserved smile,
And devoutly I kissed her white hand.

—Ah, the first flowers and their perfume!
And the murmuring spell of the sound,
The first *yes* from those lips when you so love them!

III. Après trois ans

Ayant poussé la porte étroite qui chancelle,
Je me suis promené dans le petit jardin
Qu'éclairait doucement le soleil du matin,
Pailletant chaque fleur d'une humide étincelle.

Rien n'a changé. J'ai tout revu: l'humble tonnelle
De vigne folle avec les chaises de rotin . . .
Le jet d'eau fait toujours son murmure argentin
Et le vieux tremble sa plainte sempiternelle.

Les roses comme avant palpitent; comme avant,
Les grands lys orgueilleux se balancent au vent.
Chaque alouette qui va et vient m'est connue.

Même j'ai retrouvé debout la Velléda,
Dont le plâtre s'écaille au bout de l'avenue.
—Grêle, parmi l'odeur fade du réséda.

III. After Three Years

Having pushed open the narrow wobbling gate,
I strolled around in the little garden
Gently illuminated by the morning sun
Spangling each flower with a damp flash of light.

The simple arbor: it's all still here, nothing's different,
The madly growing vines, the chairs of cane . . .
Always making its silver murmur, the fountain,
And the old aspen its perpetual lament.

Just as before, the roses throb; as before,
The huge proud lilies waver in the air.
I know every lark, coming and going.

I've even found the statue of the barbarian prophetess
Still upright down the walk, her plaster spalling,
—Slender, amid the mignonette's insipidities.

IV. Vœu

Ah! les oaristys! les premières maîtresses!
L'or des cheveux, l'azur des yeux, la fleur des chairs,
Et puis, parmi l'odeur des corps jeunes et chers,
La spontanéité craintive des caresses!

Sont-elles assez loin toutes ces allégresses
Et toutes ces candeurs! Hélas! toutes devers
Le Printemps des regrets ont fui les noirs hivers
De mes ennuis, de mes dégoûts, de mes détresses!

Si que me voilà seul à présent, morne et seul,
Morne et désespéré, plus glacé qu'un aïeul,
Et tel qu'un orphelin pauvre sans soeur aînée.

O la femme à l'amour câlin et réchauffant,
Douce, pensive et brune, et jamais étonnée,
Et qui parfois vous baise au front, comme un enfant!

IV. Wish

The first love-whispers, the first mistresses,
Blonde hair, blue eyes, the flesh in flower,
And then, amid the smell of bodies young and dear,
The timid spontaneity of caresses!

How far away it is, such happiness
And such naiveté! Alas, every reminder
Of nostalgic Spring has fled the black winter
Of my disgust, my boredom, my distress!

So that I am alone right now, gloomy and alone,
Gloomy and hopeless, like an old man chilled to the bone,
Like a poor orphan without a big sister.

O the woman whose love is tender, warming, surprised
By nothing, sweet, thoughtful, who with her dark hair
Kisses you sometimes on the forehead like a child!

V. Lassitude

A batallas de amor campo de pluma —Góngora

De la douceur, de la douceur, de la douceur!
Calme un peu ces transports fébriles, ma charmante.
Même au fort du déduit, parfois, vois-tu, l'amante
Doit avoir l'abandon paisible de la soeur.

Sois langoureuse, fais ta caresse endormante,
Bien égaux les soupirs et ton regard berceur.
Va, l'étreinte jalouse et le spasme obsesseur
Ne valent pas un long baiser, même qui mente!

Mais dans ton cher coeur d'or, me dis-tu, mon enfant,
La fauve passion va sonnant l'oliphant!...
Laisse-la trompetter à son aise, la gueuse!

Mets ton front sur mon front et ta main dans ma main,
Et fais-moi des serments que tu rompras demain,
Et pleurons jusqu'au jour, ô petite fougueuse!

V. Lassitude

For battles of love a field of down—Góngora

Softly, softly, softly, charming woman!
You must calm this feverishness a bit.
Sometimes a lover, even at pleasure's height,
Should know a peaceful sisterly abandon.

Be languorous, make your caress a doze, let
Your sighs and the lullaby of your glance be one.
The jealous clutch and the obsessing spasm, come on,
Aren't worth even one long kiss of deceit!

But in your dear gold heart, you tell me, child,
Reddish passion blows a horn of ivory coiled! . . .
Let her blow there all she wants, the trull!

Put your hand in my hand, your brow on my brow,
And make me promises you will break tomorrow,
And let us weep till daybreak, my little fireball!

VI. Mon rêve familier

Je fais souvent ce rêve étrange et pénétrant
D'une femme inconnue, et que j'aime, et qui m'aime,
Et qui n'est, chaque fois, ni tout à fait la même
Ni tout à fait une autre, et m'aime et me comprend.

Car elle me comprend, et mon coeur, transparent
Pour elle seule, hélas! cesse d'être un problème
Pour elle seule, et les moiteurs de mon front blême,
Elle seule les sait rafraîchir, en pleurant.

Est-elle brune, blonde ou rousse?—Je l'ignore.
Son nom? Je me souviens qu'il est doux et sonore,
Comme ceux des aimés que la Vie exila.

Son regard est pareil au regard des statues,
Et, pour sa voix, lointaine, et calme, et grave, elle a
L'inflexion des voix chères qui se sont tues.

VI. My Familiar Dream

Often I have this dream—a strange searching dream—
Of a woman I don't know, whom I love, and who loves me,
And who is not, each time, different, exactly,
But, loving me, understanding me, is neither the same.

Because only she understands me, and my heart, a medium
Transparent only to her, alas! stops being a problem only
For her, and the sweat from my pale forehead, only she
Can soothe it away as her own tears come.

Is she a brunette or blonde? I don't know. A redhead?
Her name? I remember it is sweet, how it resonated
Like those of loved ones since banished by Life.

Her gaze? A statue's gaze is similar.
As for her voice, it has—distant, calm, grave—
The modulation of voices gone silent, but dear.

VII. À une femme

À vous ces vers, de par la grâce consolante
De vos grands yeux où rit et pleure un rêve doux,
De par votre âme, pure et toute bonne, à vous
Ces vers du fond de ma détresse violente.

C'est qu'hélas! le hideux cauchemar qui me hante
N'a pas de trêve et va furieux, fou, jaloux,
Se multipliant comme un cortège de loups
Et se pendant après mon sort qu'il ensanglante.

Oh! je souffre, je souffre affreusement, si bien
Que le gémissement premier du premier homme
Chassé d'Éden n'est qu'une églogue au prix du mien!

Et les soucis que vous pouvez avoir sont comme
Des hirondelles sur un ciel d'après-midi,
—Chère,—par un beau jour de septembre attiédi.

VII. To a Woman

For you these lines, for the sake of the consoling grace
Where a sweet dream laughs and weeps too in your huge
Eyes, for your soul, pure and entirely good, I pledge
These lines from the bottom of my intense distress.

Because the gruesome nightmare that haunts me, alas,
Gives no quarter and in a mad jealous rage
Repeats itself like wolves in a cortege,
Dragging down my destiny it so bloodies.

Oh I suffer, I suffer frightfully, so much so that
The first groan uttered by the first man
Driven from Eden is nothing but an eclogue next to it!

And whatever cares you might have are no more than
Swallows across an afternoon sky
—Darling—on a fine lukewarm September day.

VIII. L'angoisse

Nature, rien de toi ne m'émeut, ni les champs
Nourriciers, ni l'écho vermeil des pastorales
Siciliennes, ni les pompes aurorales,
Ni la solennité dolente des couchants.

Je ris de l'Art, je ris de l'Homme aussi, des chants,
Des vers, des temples grecs et des tours en spirales
Qu'étirent dans le ciel vide les cathédrales,
Et je vois du même oeil les bons et les méchants.

Je ne crois pas en Dieu, j'abjure et je renie
Toute pensée, et quant à la vieille ironie,
L'Amour, je voudrais bien qu'on ne m'en parlât plus.

Lasse de vivre, ayant peur de mourir, pareille
Au brick perdu jouet du flux et du reflux,
Mon âme pour d'affreux naufrages appareille.

VIII. Dread

Nature, nothing in you moves me, not the nurturing
Fields, nor the ruddy echo of Sicilian pastoral,
Nor the dawn's pomp, nor the doleful
Solemnity of the sun as it is setting.

I scoff at Art, I scoff at Man also, song
And verses, Greek temples, tower stairs in spirals
Stretched into the empty sky by cathedrals,
A single glance for good and bad sufficing.

I don't believe in God, I renounce and I abjure
All thought, and as for that old irony, I conjure
That no one should speak to me of Love again.

Tired of life, afraid of death, not unlike
A lost brig, toy of ebb and flow on the ocean,
My soul weighs anchor for a frightful shipwreck.

Eaux-fortes / **Etchings**

À François Coppée / To François Coppée

I. Croquis parisien

La lune plaquait ses teintes de zinc
    Par angles obtus.
Des bouts de fumée en forme de cinq
Sortaient drus et noirs des hauts toits pointus.

Le ciel était gris, la bise pleurait
    Ainsi qu'un basson.
Au loin, un matou frileux et discret
Miaulait d'étrange et grêle façon.

Le long des maisons, escarpe et putain
    Se coulaient sans bruit,
Guettant le joueur au pas argentin
Et l'adolescent qui mord à tout fruit.

Moi, j'allais, rêvant du divin Platon
    Et de Phidias,
Et de Salamine et de Marathon,
Sous l'oeil clignotant des bleus becs de gaz.

I. Parisian Sketch

The moon plated its shades of zinc
    In blunted angles.
Shaped like a five, the wisps of smoke
Poured thick and black from the high gables.

The sky was gray. The north wind wept
    Like a bassoon.
In the distance, a shivering wary tomcat
Howled in a strange shrill fashion.

Gliding soundless, the slut and the murderer
    Lay in wait
Beside houses for the silvery step of the gambler
And the teenager who tastes every fruit.

Me, I went along dreaming of sublime Plato
    And of Pheidias,
Of Salamis and of Marathon too,
Under the flickering eye of the blue jets of gas.

II. Cauchemar

J'ai vu passer dans mon rêve
—Tel l'ouragan sur la grève,
D'une main tenant un glaive
Et de l'autre un sablier,
    Ce cavalier

Des ballades d'Allemagne
Qu'à travers ville et campagne,
Et du fleuve à la montagne,
Et des forêts au vallon,
    Un étalon

Rouge-flamme et noir d'ébène,
Sans bride, ni mors, ni rène,
Ni hop! ni cravache, entraîne
Parmi des râlements sourds
    Toujours! toujours!

Un grand feutre à longue plume
Ombrait son oeil qui s'allume
Et s'éteint. Tel, dans la brume,
Éclate et meurt l'éclair bleu
    D'une arme à feu.

Comme l'aile d'une orfraie
Qu'un subit orage effraie,
Par l'air que la neige raie,
Son manteau se soulevant
    Claquait au vent,

II. Nightmare

In my dream there hastened
—Like a tempest across the strand,
Holding an hourglass in one hand
And a sword in the other,
    This *Ritter*

Out of a ballad from Germany
Whom, across town and country,
From forest to valley,
From river to mountain,
    A stallion

Flame-red and black as ebony,
Without bridle or bit or any
Rein, no *Hop!*, no riding whip, carries away
With a smothered rattling as
    Always! always!

A great felt hat with a long feather
Shaded his eye after,
Which kindles and snuffs, rather
The way a firearm in the fog claps out
    And dies in a blue light.

Like the wing of an osprey
Frightened by the storm's sudden fury,
Through the air scored and snowy,
His cloak ballooned
    Snapping in the wind,

. . .

Et montrait d'un air de gloire
Un torse d'ombre et d'ivoire,
Tandis que dans la nuit noire
Luisaient en des cris stridents
Trente-deux dents.

.   .   .

With an air of glory to show
In the black night a torso
Made of ivory and shadow
Gleaming among shrill cries with
    Thirty-two teeth.

III. Marine

L'Océan sonore
Palpite sous l'oeil
De la lune en deuil
Et palpite encore,

Tandis qu'un éclair
Brutal et sinistre
Fend le ciel de bistre
D'un long zigzag clair,

Et que chaque lame,
En bonds convulsifs,
Le long des récifs,
Va, vient, luit et clame,

Et qu'au firmament,
Où l'ouragan erre,
Rugit le tonnerre
Formidablement.

III. Marine

The sounding ocean
Throbs beneath the eye
Of the moon veiled darkly
And throbs again,

While a violent sinister
Lightning bolt,
Its long zigzag brilliant,
Slits a sky of bister,

And each wave,
In convulsive bounds,
Goes, comes, shouts, glistens,
The length of reefs,

And in the sky
Where the tempest ranges,
The thunder roars
Terrifyingly.

IV. Effet de nuit

La nuit. La pluie. Un ciel blafard que déchiquette
De flèches et de tours à jour la silhouette
D'une ville gothique éteinte au lointain gris.
La plaine. Un gibet plein de pendus rabougris
Secoués par le bec avide des corneilles
Et dansant dans l'air noir des gigues non-pareilles,
Tandis que leurs pieds sont la pâture des loups.
Quelques buissons d'épine épars, et quelques houx
Dressant l'horreur de leur feuillage à droite, à gauche,
Sur le fuligineux fouillis d'un fond d'ébauche.
Et puis, autour de trois livides prisonniers
Qui vont pieds nus, deux cent vingt-cinq pertuisaniers
En marche, et leurs fers droits, comme des fers de herse,
Luisent à contresens des lances de l'averse.

IV. Night Effect

Night. Rain. A livid sky pierces the lacework
Of spires and towers, the silhouette of a Gothic
Town dim in the gray distance.
The plain. A gibbet full of corpses, shrivelled ones
Shaken by the crows' avid beaks,
In the black air dancing incomparable gigues
While their feet are the provender of wolves.
Some thin thorn bushes and some holly leaves
To the right and left extend the horror of their foliage
Against a background like a sooty jumbled sketch.
And then, surrounding three pale prisoners
Walking barefoot, two hundred twenty-five halberdiers,
Their shining upright weapons at cross-purposes
With the lances of the rain, like the spikes of a portcullis.

V. Grotesques

Leurs jambes pour toutes montures,
Pour tous biens l'or de leurs regards,
Par le chemin des aventures
Ils vont haillonneux et hagards.

Le sage, indigné, les harangue;
Le sot plaint ces fous hasardeux;
Les enfants leur tirent la langue
Et les filles se moquent d'eux.

C'est qu'odieux et ridicules,
Et maléfiques en effet,
Ils ont l'air, sur les crépuscules,
D'un mauvais rêve que l'on fait;

C'est que, sur leurs aigres guitares
Crispant la main des libertés,
Ils nasillent des chants bizarres,
Nostalgiques et révoltés;

C'est enfin que dans leurs prunelles
Rit et pleure—fastidieux—
L'amour des choses éternelles,
Des vieux morts et des anciens dieux!

—Donc, allez, vagabonds sans trêves,
Errez, funestes et maudits,
Le long des gouffres et des grèves,
Sous l'oeil fermé des paradis!

V. Grotesques

Conveyed by their own two legs,
All their wealth in the gold of their glance,
They travel, wild-looking, dressed in rags,
Down the avenue of incidents.

The indignant wise man harangues;
The fool pities these risky madmen;
The children stick out their tongues,
And girls mock them to scorn.

It is because, inspiring hatred, ridiculous,
A baleful influence, indeed,
They seem, in the twilight hours,
Like a bad dream someone has had;

It is because they strum
Strange songs, nostalgic, rebellious,
On their bitter guitars in freedom,
While singing through the nose;

Finally, it is because in their eyes
—Tedious—there laughs and weeps
A love of those long dead, of ancient deities,
Of things eternity keeps!

—So away with you, unresting vagabonds,
Wander, baleful and cursed, away
Down the length of chasms and strands
Under paradise's closed eye!

*   *   *

La nature à l'homme s'allie
Pour châtier comme il le faut
L'orgueilleuse mélancolie
Qui vous fait marcher le front haut.

Et, vengeant sur vous le blasphème
Des vastes espoirs véhéments,
Meurtrit votre front anathème
Au choc rude des éléments.

Les juins brûlent et les décembres
Gèlent votre chair jusqu'aux os,
Et la fièvre envahit vos membres,
Qui se déchirent aux roseaux.

Tout vous repousse et tout vous navre,
Et quand la mort viendra pour vous,
Maigre et froide, votre cadavre
Sera dédaigné par les loups!

. . .

Nature and man are one
To punish the proud melancholy
As it must be done
That makes you walk with your head held high.

And avenging on you the blasphemy
Of hopes vast and vehement,
With the rude shock of the sky
They bruise your banished front.

Junes burn, and Decembers
Freeze your flesh solid,
And fever overcomes your limbs,
Which are torn by the reeds.

Everything wounds you and pushes you away,
And when death comes for you,
Your corpse will be so cold and scrawny,
The wolves will scorn it too!

Paysages tristes / **Sad Landscapes**

À Catulle Mendès / To Catulle Mendès

I. Soleils couchants

Une aube affaiblie
Verse par les champs
La mélancolie
Des soleils couchants.
La mélancolie
Berce de doux chants
Mon coeur qui s'oublie
Aux soleils couchants.
Et d'étranges rêves,
Comme des soleils
Couchants sur les grèves,
Fantômes vermeils,
Défilent sans trêves,
Défilent, pareils
À des grands soleils
Couchants sur les grèves.

I. Sunsets

Spilled through the meadow by
An enfeebled dawn,
The melancholy
Of setting suns.
Melancholy
Rocks my heart to oblivion
With sweet melody
Amid setting suns.
And strange dreams
Like suns, setting,
Ruddy phantoms
Over shores, passing
Unceasingly, passing like some
Huge suns, like them
Over shores, setting.

II. Crépuscule du soir mystique

Le Souvenir avec le Crépuscule
Rougeoie et tremble à l'ardent horizon
De l'Espérance en flamme qui recule
Et s'agrandit ainsi qu'une cloison
Mystérieuse où mainte floraison
—Dahlia, lys, tulipe et renoncule—
S'élance autour d'un treillis, et circule
Parmi la maladive exhalaison
De parfums lourds et chauds, dont le poison
—Dahlia, lys, tulipe et renoncule—
Noyant mes sens, mon âme et ma raison,
Mêle, dans une immense pâmoison,
Le Souvenir avec le Crépuscule.

II. Mystical Dusk

Twilight together with Memory
Glows and trembles on the burning horizon
Of Hope in a flame that falls away
Then leaps up like a mysterious wall on
Which many a flower in season—
Dahlia, tulip, buttercup and lily—
Springs up a trellis, amid the unhealthy
Fragrances, the exhalation
Of heavy hot smells from which the poison—
Dahlia, tulip, buttercup and lily—
Drowning my senses, my spirit and my reason,
Mixes, in a single immense swoon,
Twilight together with Memory.

III. Promenade sentimentale

Le couchant dardait ses rayons suprêmes
Et le vent berçait les nénuphars blêmes;
Les grands nénuphars entre les roseaux,
Tristement luisaient sur les calmes eaux.
Moi j'errais tout seul, promenant ma plaie
Au long de l'étang, parmi la saulaie
Où la brume vague évoquait un grand
Fantôme laiteux se désespérant
Et pleurant avec la voix des sarcelles
Qui se rappelaient en battant des ailes
Parmi la saulaie où j'errais tout seul
Promenant ma plaie; et l'épais linceul
Des ténèbres vint noyer les suprêmes
Rayons du couchant dans ses ondes blêmes
Et des nénuphars, parmi les roseaux,
Des grands nénuphars sur les calmes eaux.

III. Sentimental Stroll

The setting sun cast its final rays
And the breeze rocked the pale water lilies;
Among the reeds, the huge water
Lilies shone sadly on the calm water.
Me, I wandered alone, walking my wound
Through the willow grove, the length of the pond
Where the vague mist conjured up some vast
Despairing milky ghost
With the voice of teals crying
As they called to each other, beating their wings
Through the willow grove where alone I wandered
Walking my wound; and the thick shroud
Of shadows came to drown the final rays
Of the setting sun in their pale waves
And, among the reeds, the water
Lilies, the huge water lilies on the calm water.

IV. Nuit du Walpurgis classique

C'est plutôt le sabbat du second Faust que l'autre.
Un rhythmique sabbat, rhythmique, extrêmement
Rhythmique.—Imaginez un jardin de Lenôtre,
    Correct, ridicule et charmant.

Des ronds-points; au milieu, des jets d'eau; des allées
Toutes droites; sylvains de marbre; dieux marins
De bronze; çà et là, des Vénus étalées;
    Des quinconces, des boulingrins;

Des châtaigniers; des plants de fleurs formant la dune;
Ici, des rosiers nains qu'un goût docte affila;
Plus loin, des ifs taillés en triangles. La lune
    D'un soir d'été sur tout cela.

Minuit sonne, et réveille au fond du parc aulique
Un air mélancolique, un sourd, lent et doux air
De chasse: tel, doux, lent, sourd et mélancolique,
    L'air de chasse de *Tannhäuser*.

Des chants voilés de cors lointains où la tendresse
Des sens étreint l'effroi de l'âme en des accords
Harmonieusement dissonnants dans l'ivresse;
    Et voici qu'à l'appel des cors

S'entrelacent soudain des formes toutes blanches,
Diaphanes, et que le clair de lune fait
Opalines parmi l'ombre verte des branches,
    —Un Watteau rêvé par Raffet!—

IV. Classic Walpurgisnacht

It's the sabbath of *Faust Part Two* rather than the other,
A rhythmical sabbath, rhythmical, extremely
Rhythmical.—Imagine a garden by Lenôtre,
    Ridiculous, charming and seemly.

A hub of paths; fountains; straight allées;
Forest gods of marble, and bronze marine
Gods; here and there, Venuses on display;
    Quincunx and bowling-green;

Chestnuts; in a hillock, seedling flowers;
Here, dwarf rose bushes pruned by a learnèd taste;
Further off, the yews' topiary isosceles.
    Over all of this, the moonlight of August.

Midnight strikes, and wakes in the depths of the royal
Park a melancholy air, a heavy, slow and sweet air,
A hunter's air, sweet, slow, heavy, melancholy, comparable
    To the hunter's air from *Tannhäuser*.

Husky songs of distant horns, in which the tenderness
Of the senses clasps the terror of the soul in intervals
Harmoniously dissonant in their drunkenness;
    And there, in response to the horns' call,

White shapes suddenly intertwine,
Translucent, which, amid the green shadow
Of branches, the moonlight makes opaline
    —Raffet's dream of Watteau!—

. . .

S'entrelacent parmi l'ombre verte des arbres
D'un geste alangui, plein d'un désespoir profond;
Puis, autour des massifs, des bronzes et des marbres
     Très lentement dansent en rond.

—Ces spectres agités, sont-ce donc la pensée
Du poète ivre, ou son regret, ou son remords,
Ces spectres agités en tourbe cadencée,
     Ou bien tout simplement des morts?

Sont-ce donc ton remords, ô rêvasseur qu'invite
L'horreur, ou ton regret, ou ta pensée,—hein?—tous
Ces spectres qu'un vertige irrésistible agite,
     Ou bien des morts qui seraient fous?—

N'importe! ils vont toujours, les fébriles fantômes,
Menant leur ronde vaste et morne et tressautant
Comme dans un rayon de soleil des atomes,
     Et s'évaporent à l'instant

Humide et blême où l'aube éteint l'un après l'autre
Les cors, en sorte qu'il ne reste absolument
Plus rien—absolument—qu'un jardin de Lenôtre,
     Correct, ridicule et charmant.

. . .

Intertwine amid the trees' green shadow
With a languid gesture, full of a deep despair;
Then dancing in a circle, very slow,
    Around the shrubs, the bronze and marble sculpture.

—These restless ghosts, are they the thinking
Of the drunken poet, his regret, his remorse, or instead,
These restless ghosts in a rhythmical throng,
    Are they simply the dead?

Is it your remorse, o dreamer,
That conjures this horror, or your regret, or your thought,—eh?—
All these ghosts restless with a compelling fever,
Or is it the dead who would be crazy?—

It doesn't matter! Always these feverish phantoms
Leading their vast round dance, sad and tossing
Like dust-motes caught in sunbeams,
    In a damp pallid moment disappearing

When dawn extinguishes the horns one after the other,
So that there remains absolutely
Nothing more—absolutely—than a garden by Lenôtre,
    ridiculous, charming and seemly.

V. Chanson d'automne

Les sanglots longs
Des violons
  De l'automne
Blessent mon coeur
D'une langueur
  Monotone.

Tout suffocant
Et blême, quand
  Sonne l'heure,
Je me souviens
Des jours anciens
  Et je pleure;

Et je m'en vais
Au vent mauvais
  Qui m'emporte
Deçà, delà,
Pareil à la
  Feuille morte.

V. Autumn Song

The long sobbing
Of autumn strings,
   Grievous,
Wounds my heart
With a languor that
   Is monotonous.

Stifled
And pallid
   When the hour rings,
I summon
Days long gone
   With my weeping;

And then I go
On an ill wind to
   Carry me off
Here and there
In just the manner
   Of a dead leaf.

VI. L'heure du berger

La lune est rouge au brumeux horizon;
Dans un brouillard qui danse, la prairie
S'endort fumeuse, et la grenouille crie
Par les joncs verts où circule un frisson;

Les fleurs des eaux referment leurs corolles,
Des peupliers profilent aux lointains,
Droits et serrés, leurs spectres incertains;
Vers les buissons errent les lucioles;

Les chats-huants s'éveillent, et sans bruit
Rament l'air noir avec leurs ailes lourdes,
Et le zénith s'emplit de lueurs sourdes.
Blanche, Vénus émerge, et c'est la Nuit.

VI. Evening Star

On the misty horizon the moon is red;
The meadow, in a shifting fog,
Dozes smokily, and the frog
Calls from the shivering green reed;

The water flowers again close their faces;
The poplars are in silhouette far away,
Their dim shapes straight and set closely;
Toward the thicket wander fireflies;

The barn owls awaken and, silent,
Oar the black air with their heavy wings,
And the zenith fills with dull glimmerings.
Pale Venus rises, and it is night.

VII. Le rossignol

Comme un vol criard d'oiseaux en émoi,
Tous mes souvenirs s'abattent sur moi,
S'abattent parmi le feuillage jaune
De mon coeur mirant son tronc plié d'aune
Au tain violet de l'eau des Regrets,
Qui mélancoliquement coule auprès,
S'abattent, et puis la rumeur mauvaise
Qu'une brise moite en montant apaise,
S'éteint par degrés dans l'arbre, si bien
Qu'au bout d'un instant on n'entend plus rien,
Plus rien que la voix célébrant l'Absente,
Plus rien que la voix,—ô si languissante!—
De l'oiseau qui fut mon Premier Amour,
Et qui chante encor comme au premier jour;
Et, dans la splendeur triste d'une lune
Se levant blafarde et solennelle, une
Nuit mélancolique et lourde d'été,
Pleine de silence et d'obscurité,
Berce sur l'azur qu'un vent doux effleure
L'arbre qui frissonne et l'oiseau qui pleure.

VII. The Nightingale

Like a troubled flock of birds when they cry,
All my memories fall on me,
They fall amid the yellow leaves of my heart
Gazing at its alder trunk, bent
In the silver mirror-back of the water
Of Regret that flows melancholy and near,
They fall, and the evil murmur that is
Calmed by the rise of a sticky breeze
Is subdued bit by bit in the woods so well
That after a moment one hears nothing at all,
Nothing more than the voice that is extolling
The Absent, nothing more—o so languishing!—
Than the voice of my First Love, the bird
Singing still as on that first day it did;
And in the sad splendor of a moon
Rising pallid and solemn,
A heavy melancholy night in summer,
Full of silence and what is obscure,
Rocks on the azure a breeze brushes with fingertips
The tree that trembles and the bird that weeps.

Caprices / **Caprices**

À Henry Winter / *To Henry Winter*

I. Femme et chatte

Elle jouait avec sa chatte,
Et c'était merveille de voir
La main blanche et la blanche patte
S'ébattre dans l'ombre du soir.

Elle cachait—la scélérate!—
Sous ces mitaines de fil noir
Ses meurtriers ongles d'agate,
Coupants et clairs comme un rasoir.

L'autre aussi faisait la sucrée
Et rentrait sa griffe acérée,
Mais le diable n'y perdait rien . . .

Et dans le boudoir où, sonore,
Tintait son rire aérien,
Brillaient quatre points de phosphore.

I. Woman and Pussy

She was playing with her pussycat,
And to see it was a wonder:
The white hand and the paw, white,
Romp in the night's umber.

She concealed—the skank!—
Her agate nails of murder
Beneath those half-gloves' black,
Cutting and bright as a razor.

She was all sweetness too, the other one,
And drew in her steel talon,
But the devil lost nothing by waiting ...

And in the boudoir as, tuned
And aerial, her laughter rang,
Four points of phosphor burned.

II. Jésuitisme

Le chagrin qui me tue est ironique, et joint
Le sarcasme au supplice, et ne torture point
Franchement, mais picote avec un faux sourire
Et transforme en spectacle amusant mon martyre,
Et sur la bière où gît mon Rêve mi-pourri,
Beugle un *De profundis* sur l'air du *Traderi*.
C'est un Tartufe qui, tout en mettant des roses
Pompons sur les autels des Madones moroses,
Tout en faisant chanter à des enfants de choeur
Ces cantiques d'eau tiède où se baigne le coeur,
Tout en amidonnant ces guimpes amoureuses
Qui serpentent au coeur sacré des Bienheureuses,
Tout en disant à voix basse son chapelet,
Tout en passant la main sur son petit collet,
Tout en parlant avec componction de l'âme,
N'en médite pas moins ma ruine,—l'infâme!

II. Jesuitism

The ill humor that kills me is ironic, and blends
Sarcasm and anguish, and never torments
Honestly, but stings me with a false smile
And changes my agony into an amusing spectacle,
And on the bier where my half-rotten Dream lies,
To the tune of *Traderi* it roars out a *De profundis*.
It is a Tartuffe who, while arranging pompon
Roses around the altars of sullen
Madonnas, while making choirboys sing
Hymns like lukewarm water for the heart's bathing,
While starching those loving chemisettes
That wind around the sacred heart of the Blessed,
While telling the rosary in a low voice, or
While raising a hand toward his little collar,
While speaking with a great show of dignity of the soul,
Ponders no less my ruin,—unspeakable!

III. La chanson des ingénues

Nous sommes les Ingénues
Aux bandeaux plats, à l'oeil bleu,
Qui vivons, presque inconnues,
Dans les romans qu'on lit peu.

Nous allons entrelacées,
Et le jour n'est pas plus pur
Que le fond de nos pensées,
Et nos rêves sont d'azur;

Et nous courons par les prées
Et rions et babillons
Des aubes jusqu'aux vesprées,
Et chassons aux papillons;

Et des chapeaux de bergères
Défendent notre fraîcheur,
Et nos robes—si légères—
Sont d'une extrême blancheur;

Les Richelieux, les Caussades
Et les chevaliers Faublas
Nous prodiguent les oeillades,
Les saluts et les «hélas!»

Mais en vain, et leurs mimiques
Se viennent casser le nez
Devant les plis ironiques
De nos jupons détournés;

III. The Song of the Ingenues

We are the Ingenues,
Our hair straight-parted, blue-eyed,
Who live, hardly known,
In novels one doesn't much read.

We go arm in arm,
And day itself is not more pure
Than our thoughts are, at bottom,
And our dreams are azure;

And we run through the meadows
With babbling and titters,
And we chase butterflies
From dawn until vespers,

Our shepherdess' bonnets
Protect our freshness,
And our frocks—almost transparent—
Are of an extreme whiteness;

The Richelieus, the Caussades
And the knights Faublas
Lavish their oeillades,
Salutations and "alases!"

But in vain, and their exaggerated
Gestures go down to defeat
Before the ironic folds
Of our flouncing skirts;

. . .

Et notre candeur se raille
Des imaginations
De ces raseurs de muraille,
Bien que parfois nous sentions

Battre nos coeurs sous nos mantes
À des pensers clandestins,
En nous sachant les amantes
Futures des libertins.

. . .

And our naiveté mocks at all
The fantasy
Of those who hug the walls,
Even if we feel occasionally

Beneath the cloak our hearts race
With clandestine
Thoughts, knowing ourselves the future lovers
Of libertines.

IV. Une grande dame

Belle «à damner les saints», à troubler sous l'aumusse
Un vieux juge! Elle marche impérialement,
Elle parle—et ses dents font un miroitement—
Italien, avec un léger accent russe.

Ses yeux froids où l'émail sertit le bleu de Prusse
Ont l'éclat insolent et dur du diamant.
Pour la splendeur du sein, pour le rayonnement
De la peau, nulle reine ou courtisane, fût-ce

Cléopâtre la lynce ou la chatte Ninon,
N'égale sa beauté patricienne, non!
Vois, ô bon Buridan: «C'est une grande dame!»

Il faut—pas de milieu!—l'adorer à genoux,
Plat, n'ayant d'astre aux cieux que ces lourds cheveux roux
Ou bien lui cravacher la face, à cette femme!

IV. A Great Lady

So beautiful that she would "tempt the saints,"
Or trouble an old judge beneath his gown!
Like an empress she walks and—like a mirror her teeth shine—
Speaks Italian with a slight Russian accent.

Her cold eyes, Prussian blue set in enamel,
Have the insolent hard luster of diamonds.
The splendor of her breast, the radiance
Of her skin, no queen or courtesan can equal,

Neither kittenish Ninon nor lynx-like Cleopatra,
None can match her patrician beauty, no!
You know it, good Buridan: "These are great ladies!"

You must—no middle ground!—on your knees worship her,
Prostrate, no star in the heavens but her heavy red hair,
Or else horsewhip this woman in the face!

V. Monsieur Prudhomme

Il est grave: il est maire et père de famille.
Son faux col engloutit son oreille. Ses yeux,
Dans un rêve sans fin, flottent insoucieux
Et le printemps en fleurs sur ses pantoufles brille.

Que lui fait l'astre d'or, que lui fait la charmille
Où l'oiseau chante à l'ombre, et que lui font les cieux,
Et les prés verts et les gazons silencieux?
Monsieur Prudhomme songe à marier sa fille

Avec monsieur Machin, un jeune homme cossu.
Il est juste-milieu, botaniste et pansu.
Quant aux faiseurs de vers, ces vauriens, ces maroufles,

Ces fainéants barbus, mal peignés, il les a
Plus en horreur que son éternel coryza,
Et le printemps en fleurs brille sur ses pantoufles.

V. Mister Wiseman

He is solemn: he is a mayor and the family's father.
His detachable collar swallows his ear. His eyes swim
Unconcerned in an endless dream
And flowering spring shines on his slippers.

What is the golden star to him, what is the arbor
Where the bird sings in the shade, what to him
Are skies and green meadows and lawns' calm?
Mister Wiseman considers marrying his daughter

To Mister Whatsit, politically middle-of-the-road,
A young man of means, a botanist, potbellied.
As for these rogues and good-for-nothing

Versifiers, these bearded idlers dressed so ill,
He dreads them more than his head cold, which is perpetual,
And on his slippers shines flowering spring.

Autres poèmes / **Other Poems**

Initium

Les violons mêlaient leur rire au chant des flûtes,
Et le bal tournoyait quand je la vis passer
Avec ses cheveux blonds jouant sur les volutes
De son oreille où mon Désir comme un baiser
S'élançait et voulait lui parler sans oser.

Cependant elle allait, et la mazurque lente
La portait dans son rythme indolent comme un vers,
—Rime mélodieuse, image étincelante,—
Et son âme d'enfant rayonnait à travers
La sensuelle ampleur de ses yeux gris et verts.

Et depuis, ma Pensée—immobile—contemple
Sa Splendeur évoquée, en adoration,
Et, dans son Souvenir, ainsi que dans un temple,
Mon Amour entre, plein de superstition.

Et je crois que voici venir la Passion.

Initium

With the song of the flutes the violins mingled their laughter,
And the dance spun around me when I saw her pass,
Her blonde hair playing on the whorl of her ear
Where my Desire darted like a kiss
And wanted to speak to her but did not dare this.

Yet it seemed that the slow mazurka, in her going,
Carried her in its languid rhythm like a verse,
—Rhyme melodious, image dazzling—
and her child's soul was
shining through the sensual fullness of her gray-green eyes.

And ever since, my Thought gazes—immobile—
At her recalled Splendor, in adoration,
And into the Memory of it, as if into a temple,
My Love enters, full of superstition.

And I believe that it is coming, Passion.

Çavitrî (*Mahabharata*)

Pour sauver son époux, Çavitri fit le vœu
De se tenir trois jours entiers, trois nuits entières,
Debout, sans remuer jambes, buste ou paupières:
Rigide, ainsi que dit Vyaça, comme un pieu.

Ni, Çurya, tes rais cruels, ni la langueur
Que Tchandra vient épandre à minuit sur les cimes
Ne firent défaillir, dans leurs efforts sublimes,
La pensée et la chair de la femme au grand coeur.

—Que nous cerne l'Oubli, noir et morne assassin,
Ou que l'Envie aux traits amers nous ait pour cibles,
Ainsi que Çavitri faisons-nous impassibles,
Mais, comme elle, dans l'âme ayons un haut dessein.

Savitri (*Mahabharata*)

To save her husband, Savitri promised
To stand upright for three whole nights, three whole days,
Her legs, her chest, even her eyelids motionless:
Stiff, according to Vyasa, as a post.

Neither, Surya, your cruel rays, nor the languor
That Chandra spreads at midnight on the peaks
Could by their sublime effort once make weak
This woman great-hearted in flesh and idea.

—Let Oblivion surround us, black and gloomy assassin,
Or let bitter Longing make us its target,
Like Savitri let us be impassive, yet
Like her, in our soul let us bear a great design.

Sub Urbe

Les petits ifs du cimetière
Frémissent au vent hiémal,
Dans la glaciale lumière.

Avec des bruits sourds qui font mal,
Les croix de bois des tombes neuves
Vibrent sur un ton anormal.

Silencieux comme les fleuves,
Mais gros de pleurs comme eux de flots,
Les fils, les mères et les veuves,

Par les détours du triste enclos,
S'écoulent,—lente théorie,—
Au rythme heurté des sanglots.

Le sol sous les pieds glisse et crie,
Là-haut de grands nuages tors
S'échevèlent avec furie.

Pénétrant comme le remords,
Tombe un froid lourd qui vous écoeure,
Et qui doit filtrer chez les morts,

Chez les pauvres morts, à toute heure
Seuls, et sans cesse grelottants,
—Qu'on les oublie ou qu'on les pleure!—

Sub Urbe

The cemetery's small yews
Tremble in the glacial light,
In the wintry breeze.

With muffled sounds that hurt,
On the new graves wooden crosses
Irregularly vibrate.

Silently as rivers,
But swollen with tears like a flood,
The sons, the widows and mothers,

Along the curves of the sad
Enclosure—in a slow cortège—disperse,
To the rhythm of sobs interrupted.

The earth beneath their feet slips and cries,
While huge twisted clouds overhead
Wildly dishevel themselves.

Piercing as remorse, a heavy cold
Descends that sickens you,
And that must seep down to the dead,

To the poor dead who
Are always alone and shivering
Endlessly—Whether we forget them or are able to

. . .

Ah! vienne vite le Printemps,
Et son clair soleil qui caresse,
Et ses doux oiseaux caquetants!

Refleurisse l'enchanteresse
Gloire des jardins et des champs
Que l'âpre hiver tient en détresse!

Et que,—des levers aux couchants,—
L'or dilaté d'un ciel sans bornes
Berce de parfums et de chants,

Chers endormis, vos sommeils mornes!

. . .

Weep for them!—Ah, let the Spring
Come quickly, and its bright sun that caresses
And its sweet birds' babbling!

Let flower again the enchanting glories
Of the gardens and the fields that
Bitter winter keeps in distress!

And let,—from sunrise to sunset,—
The spread gold of a sky that is boundless
Rock with its songs and its scents

Your dismal sleep, dear sleepers!

Sérénade

Comme la voix d'un mort qui chanterait
    Du fond de sa fosse,
Maîtresse, entends monter vers ton retrait
    Ma voix aigre et fausse.

Ouvre ton âme et ton oreille au son
    De ma mandoline:
Pour toi j'ai fait, pour toi, cette chanson
    Cruelle et câline.

Je chanterai tes yeux d'or et d'onyx
    Purs de toutes ombres,
Puis le Léthé de ton sein, puis le Styx
    De tes cheveux sombres.

Comme la voix d'un mort qui chanterait
    Du fond de sa fosse,
Maîtresse, entends monter vers ton retrait
    Ma voix aigre et fausse.

Puis je louerai beaucoup, comme il convient,
    Cette chair bénie
Dont le parfum opulent me revient
    Les nuits d'insomnie.

Et pour finir, je dirai le baiser
    De ta lèvre rouge,
Et ta douceur à me martyriser,
    —Mon Ange!—ma Gouge!

Serenade

Like the voice of a corpse who would sing
    From the bottom of the pit,
Mistress, hear my voice, bitter, false, rising
    Toward your retreat.

Open your ear to the sound, open your soul
    To my mandolin:
I made it for you, caressing and cruel,
    For you this tune.

I will sing of your eyes' gold and onyx
    Unshadowed, pure,
Then the Lethe of your bosom, then the Styx
    Of your dark hair.

Like the voice of a corpse who would sing
    From the bottom of the pit,
Mistress, hear my voice, bitter, false, rising
    Toward your retreat.

Then, meet and right, I will magnify
    This blessèd flesh, its
Rich savor, that comes back to me
    On sleepless nights.

And finally I will tell of the kiss
    Of your red lip,
And what martyrs me, your sweetness,
    My Angel!—My Tramp!

. . .

Ouvre ton âme et ton oreille au son
   De ma mandoline:
Pour toi j'ai fait, pour toi, cette chanson
   Cruelle et câline.

. . .

Open your ear to the sound, open your soul
   To the mandolin:
I made it for you, caressing and cruel,
   For you this tune.

Un dahlia

Courtisane au sein dur, à l'oeil opaque et brun
S'ouvrant avec lenteur comme celui d'un boeuf,
Ton grand torse reluit ainsi qu'un marbre neuf.

Fleur grasse et riche, autour de toi ne flotte aucun
Arôme, et la beauté sereine de ton corps
Déroule, mate, ses impeccables accords.

Tu ne sens même pas la chair, ce goût qu'au moins
Exhalent celles-là qui vont fanant les foins,
Et tu trônes, Idole insensible à l'encens.

—Ainsi le Dahlia, roi vêtu de splendeur,
Élève, sans orgueil, sa tête sans odeur,
Irritant au milieu des jasmins agaçants!

A Dahlia

Hard-breasted courtesan, your eye opaque and brown,
Opening like an ox's eye, that slow,
It gleams like fresh-cut marble, your big torso.

Rich fat flower, no aroma, none,
Hovers around you, and your body's serene beauty
Spins out its matte and perfect harmonies.

You don't even smell of flesh, that whiff exhaled
at least by those who go tedding hay in the field,
And you lord it, Idol indifferent to incense.

—Just as the Dahlia, a king arrayed in splendor,
Raises its proud head, but without odor,
Irritating amid the seductive jessamines!

Nevermore

Allons, mon pauvre coeur, allons, *mon vieux complice,*
Redresse et peins à neuf tous tes arcs triomphaux;
Brûle un encens ranci sur tes autels d'or faux;
Sème de fleurs les bords béants du précipice;
Allons, mon pauvre coeur, allons, *mon vieux complice!*

Pousse à Dieu ton cantique, ô chantre rajeuni;
Entonne, orgue enroué, des *Te Deum* splendides;
Vieillard prématuré, mets du fard sur tes rides:
Couvre-toi de tapis mordorés, mur jauni;
Pousse à Dieu ton cantique, ô chantre rajeuni.

Sonnez, grelots; sonnez, clochettes; sonnez, cloches!
Car mon rêve impossible a pris corps, et je l'ai
Entre mes bras pressé: le Bonheur, cet ailé
Voyageur qui de l'Homme évite les approches.
—Sonnez, grelots; sonnez, clochettes; sonnez, cloches!

Le Bonheur a marché côte à côte avec moi;
Mais la FATALITÉ ne connaît point de trêve:
Le ver est dans le fruit, le réveil dans le rêve,
Et le remords est dans l'amour: telle est la loi.
—Le Bonheur a marché côte à côte avec moi.

Nevermore

Let's go, my poor heart, let's go, *my old accomplice,*
Your triumphal arches, let them be repainted and righted;
Burn stale incense on your altars of false gold;
Sow flowers along the yawning edges of the precipice;
Let's go, my poor heart, let's go, *my old accomplice!*

Raise to God, o rejuvenated bard, your canticle;
Strike up your splendid *Te Deums*, hoarse organ;
Old before your time, wrinkled, slap some rouge on:
Cover yourself with rich brown carpets, yellowed wall;
Raise to God, o rejuvenated bard, your canticle.

Ring, round bells; ring, little bells; bells, ring on!
For my impossible dream has been embodied,
And I have held it in my arms: Happiness, this winged
Traveler who avoids the approach of Man.
—Ring, round bells; ring, little bells; bells, ring on!

Happiness walked side by side with me;
But FATALITY knows no respite:
Waking is in the dream, the worm is in the fruit,
Remorse is in love: that is how it must be.
—Happiness walked side by side with me.

Il bacio

Baiser! rose trémière au jardin des caresses!
Vif accompagnement sur le clavier des dents
Des doux refrains qu'Amour chante en les coeurs ardents,
Avec sa voix d'archange aux langueurs charmeresses!

Sonore et gracieux Baiser, divin Baiser!
Volupté non pareille, ivresse inénarrable!
Salut! L'homme, penché sur ta coupe adorable,
S'y grise d'un bonheur qu'il ne sait épuiser.

Comme le vin du Rhin et comme la musique,
Tu consoles et tu berces, et le chagrin
Expire avec la moue en ton pli purpurin...
Qu'un plus grand, Goethe ou Will, te dresse un vers classique.

Moi, je ne puis, chétif trouvère de Paris,
T'offrir que ce bouquet de strophes enfantines:
Sois bénin et, pour prix, sur les lèvres mutines
D'Une que je connais, Baiser, descends, et ris.

Il bacio

Kiss! Hollyhock in the garden of caresses!
Lively accompaniment on the keyboard of the teeth
To the soft refrains that Love sings in passionate hearts with
Its archangel's voice to enchanting languidness!

Resonant and graceful Kiss, heavenly Kiss!
Nonpareil voluptuousness, intoxication indescribable!
All hail! The man, bent over your adorable
Cup, gets drunk there with an inexhaustible happiness.

As by music, as by a Rhine wine,
You cradle us and we are consoled,
And sorrow expires with a pout in your crimson fold . . .
Let a greater one, Goethe or Will, write you a classic line.

Me, I can't do it, this bouquet of childish strophes
Is all I can offer, a sickly trouvère of Paris:
Be kind and, to reward me, come down on the mischievous
Lips of One I know, Kiss, and laugh.

Dans les bois

D'autres,—des innocents ou bien des lymphatiques,—
Ne trouvent dans les bois que charmes langoureux,
Souffles frais et parfums tièdes. Ils sont heureux!
D'autres s'y sentent pris—rêveurs—d'effrois mystiques.

Ils sont heureux! Pour moi, nerveux, et qu'un remords
Épouvantable et vague affole sans relâche,
Par les forêts je tremble à la façon d'un lâche
Qui craindrait une embûche ou qui verrait des morts.

Ces grands rameaux jamais apaisés, comme l'onde,
D'où tombe un noir silence avec une ombre encor
Plus noire, tout ce morne et sinistre décor
Me remplit d'une horreur triviale et profonde.

Surtout les soirs d'été: la rougeur du couchant
Se fond dans le gris bleu des brumes qu'elle teinte
D'incendie et de sang; et l'angélus qui tinte
Au lointain semble un cri plaintif se rapprochant.

Le vent se lève chaud et lourd, un frisson passe
Et repasse, toujours plus fort, dans l'épaisseur
Toujours plus sombre des hauts chênes, obsesseur,
Et s'éparpille, ainsi qu'un miasme, dans l'espace.

La nuit vient. Le hibou s'envole. C'est l'instant
Où l'on songe aux récits des aïeules naïves . . .
Sous un fourré, là-bas, là-bas, des sources vives
Font un bruit d'assassins postés se concertant.

In the Woods

Those who are simple or phlegmatic—others—
Find in the forest languid pleasures only,
Cool breezes, tepid smells. They are happy!
Others are overcome there—dreamers—by mystical terrors.

They are happy! For nervous me, whom a vague appalling remorse
Throws into a state of relentless panic,
I quiver through the forest like
A coward afraid of an ambush or seeing a corpse.

These huge branches that are never pacified,
Like a wave from which a black silence falls with a shadow
Even blacker, all this gloomy and appalling scenario
Fills me with a horror both mundane and profound.

Especially summer evenings: the sunset's reddening
Fades away into the gray blue of mists that it tinges
With fire and with blood; and the ringing of the angelus
In the distance sounds like a plaintive cry approaching.

The wind rises, hot and heavy, a shudder passes
And passes again, always more strongly, through the depth
Always darker of the high oaks, obsessive,
And scatters, like a miasma, through space.

Night comes. The owl flies. It is the moment when
One thinks about old wives' tales . . .
Under a thicket, over there, over there, a spring spills,
Making a noise like the plotting of assassins.

Nocturne parisien

À Edmond Lepelletier

Roule, roule ton flot indolent, morne Seine.—
Sous tes ponts qu'environne une vapeur malsaine
Bien des corps ont passé, morts, horribles, pourris,
Dont les âmes avaient pour meurtrier Paris.
Mais tu n'en traînes pas, en tes ondes glacées,
Autant que ton aspect m'inspire de pensées!

Le Tibre a sur ses bords des ruines qui font
Monter le voyageur vers un passé profond,
Et qui, de lierre noir et de lichen couvertes,
Apparaissent, tas gris, parmi les herbes vertes.
Le gai Guadalquivir rit aux blonds orangers
Et reflète, les soirs, des boléros légers,
Le Pactole a son or, le Bosphore a sa rive
Où vient faire son kief l'odalisque lascive.
Le Rhin est un burgrave, et c'est un troubadour
Que le Lignon, et c'est un ruffian que l'Adour.
Le Nil, au bruit plaintif de ses eaux endormies,
Berce de rêves doux le sommeil des momies.
Le grand Meschascébé, fier de ses joncs sacrés,
Charrie augustement ses îlots mordorés,
Et soudain, beau d'éclairs, de fracas et de fastes,
Splendidement s'écroule en Niagaras vastes.
L'Eurotas, où l'essaim des cygnes familiers
Mêle sa grâce blanche au vert mat des lauriers,
Sous son ciel clair que raie un vol de gypaète,
Rhythmique et caressant, chante ainsi qu'un poète.
Enfin, Ganga, parmi les hauts palmiers tremblants
Et les rouges padmas, marche à pas fiers et lents

Parisian Nocturne

To Edmond Lepelletier

Wheel on, dismal Seine, wheel on in sluggish waves—
Under your bridges that an unwholesome mist wreathes,
Many bodies have drifted, dead, rotten, horrible,
With Paris for the murderer of their soul.
Still you have carried off fewer, in your icy freshets,
Than what you have inspired in me, these thoughts!

The Tiber has ruins that make
The traveler climb toward the deep past on each bank,
And that, covered with lichen and black ivy,
Appear among green weeds, a heap of gray.
Glad Guadalquivir laughs amid gold citrus
And, evenings, mirrors the light boleros.
The Pactolus has its gold, the Bosporus its coast
Where the lascivious odalisque comes at midday to rest.
The Rhine's a burgrave, and a troubadour
The Lignon, and a rogue the Adour.
The Nile, to its sluggish water's plaintive noise,
Rocks with soft dreams the sleep of mummies.
The great Mississippi, proud of its sacred reeds,
Majestically bears its bronze islets onward,
And suddenly, handsome with lightning flashes, pomp and fracas,
Falls splendidly in huge Niagaras.
The Eurotas, where the bevy of familiar swans
Mingles its white grace with the laurel's dull green
Beneath a bright sky scored by the vultures' kettle,
Sings like a poet, caressing, rhythmical.
At last the Ganges, amid tall trembling
Palms and red lotus, with proud slow steps going

En appareil royal, tandis qu'au loin la foule
Le long des temples va, hurlant, vivante houle,
Au claquement massif des cymbales de bois,
Et qu'accroupi, filant ses notes de hautbois,
Du saut de l'antilope agile attendant l'heure,
Le tigre jaune au dos rayé s'étire et pleure.

—Toi, Seine, tu n'as rien. Deux quais, et voilà tout,
Deux quais crasseux, semés de l'un à l'autre bout
D'affreux bouquins moisis et d'une foule insigne
Qui fait dans l'eau des ronds et qui pêche à la ligne.
Oui, mais quand vient le soir, raréfiant enfin
Les passants alourdis de sommeil ou de faim,
Et que le couchant met au ciel des taches rouges,
Qu'il fait bon aux rêveurs descendre de leurs bouges
Et, s'accoudant au pont de la Cité, devant
Notre-Dame, songer, coeur et cheveux au vent!
Les nuages, chassés par la brise nocturne,
Courent, cuivreux et roux, dans l'azur taciturne.
Sur la tête d'un roi du portail, le soleil,
Au moment de mourir, pose un baiser vermeil.
L'Hirondelle s'enfuit à l'approche de l'ombre,
Et l'on voit voleter la chauve-souris sombre.
Tout bruit s'apaise autour. A peine un vague son
Dit que la ville est là qui chante sa chanson,
Qui lèche ses tyrans et qui mord ses victimes;
Et c'est l'aube des vols, des amours et des crimes.
—Puis, tout à coup, ainsi qu'un ténor effaré
Lançant dans l'air bruni son cri désespéré,

Royally arrayed, while a crowd in the distance with a yell
Swarms the length of temples, a living swell,
To the wooden cymbals' huge chattering,
And squats, drawing out the oboe's notes, waiting
For the hour that the lithe antelope leaps,
The yellow tiger with the striped back stretches and weeps.

—You, Seine, you have nothing. Two quais, nothing more,
Two filthy quais spread from one end to the other
With horrid moldy books and a crowd of distinction
Skims pebbles in the water and fishes with a line.
Yes, but when evening comes finally to rarefy
Those passersby whom sleep or hunger has made heavy,
And when the sky is stained red with sunset,
Then it is good for dreamers to come down from their tenement,
And on the pont de la Cité resting their elbows,
In front of Notre-Dame to muse, hearts and hair in the breeze!
Clouds that the breezes of evening pursue
Scud, coppery and reddish, in the silent blue.
On the head of a king on the portal, the sun bestows,
At the moment of death, a vermilion kiss.
The swallow flees at the approach of night,
And one sees the dark bat flit about.
Noise dies down all around. A vague sound barely
Suggests that it is there singing its song, the city,
Licking its tyrants, biting its victims;
And it is a new dawn for thefts, love and crimes.
—Then all of a sudden, like a startled tenor
Flinging his desperate cry through the darkened air,

Son cri qui se lamente, et se prolonge, et crie,
Éclate en quelque coin l'orgue de Barbarie:
Il brame un de ces airs, romances ou polkas,
Qu'enfants nous tapotions sur nos harmonicas
Et qui font, lents ou vifs, réjouissants ou tristes,
Vibrer l'âme aux proscrits, aux femmes, aux artistes.
C'est écorché, c'est faux, c'est horrible, c'est dur,
Et donnerait la fièvre à Rossini, pour sûr;
Ces rires sont traînés, ces plaintes sont hachées;
Sur une clef de sol impossible juchées,
Les notes ont un rhume et les *do* sont des *la*,
Mais qu'importe! l'on pleure en entendant cela!
Mais l'esprit, transporté dans le pays des rêves,
Sent à ces vieux accords couler en lui des sèves;
La pitié monte au coeur et les larmes aux yeux,
Et l'on voudrait pouvoir goûter la paix des cieux,
Et dans une harmonie étrange et fantastique
Qui tient de la musique et tient de la plastique,
L'âme, les inondant de lumière et de chant,
Mêle les sons de l'orgue aux rayons du couchant!

—Et puis l'orgue s'éloigne, et puis c'est le silence,
Et la nuit terne arrive et Vénus se balance
Sur une molle nue au fond des cieux obscurs:
On allume les becs de gaz le long des murs.
Et l'astre et les flambeaux font des zigzags fantasques
Dans le fleuve plus noir que le velours des masques;
Et le contemplateur sur le haut garde-fou
Par l'air et par les ans rouillé comme un vieux sou

His cry that bewails and cries and carries on,
From somewhere there breaks out a barrel organ:
It bawls out one of its tunes, romances or polkas
That as kids we used to tap out on our harmonicas,
The ones that, joyful or sad, slow or fast,
Stir the soul of exiles, women, artists.
It's flayed, it's false, it's horrible, it's hard,
for sure it would make Rossini grow fevered;
These laments are hacked, and forced these laughs;
Perched on an impossible treble clef,
The notes have a cold, the *do* is the *la*,
But who cares? One weeps, hearing it, anyway!
Carried to the land of dreams, the spirit
Feels the sap flow, listening to tunes so ancient;
Pity rises to the heart, tears to the eyes,
And one would like to be able to taste the heavens' peace,
And in a melody strange and fantastic
That has in it something of music and of a more plastic
Art, the soul, flooding them with song and with light,
Mingles the sounds of the hurdy-gurdy with the rays of the sunset!

—And then the barrel-organ grows fainter, and it is
Silent, and lifeless night arrives, and Venus wavers
On a soft cloud at the bottom of dark skies:
Along the walls are lit the jets of gas.
And the star and the torches make weird zigzags
In a river blacker than the velvet of masks;
And the one high above it musing on,
The guard rail rusted by the breeze and the years like an old coin,

Se penche, en proie aux vents néfastes de l'abîme.
Pensée, espoir serein, ambition sublime,
Tout, jusqu'au souvenir, tout s'envole, tout fuit,
Et l'on est seul avec Paris, l'Onde et la Nuit!

—Sinistre trinité! De l'ombre dures portes!
Mané-Thécel-Pharès des illusions mortes!
Vous êtes toutes trois, ô Goules de malheur,
Si terribles, que l'Homme, ivre de la douleur
Que lui font en perçant sa chair vos doigts de spectre,
L'Homme, espèce d'Oreste à qui manque une Électre,
Sous la fatalité de votre regard creux
Ne peut rien et va droit au précipice affreux;
Et vous êtes aussi toutes trois si jalouses
De tuer et d'offrir au grand Ver des épouses
Qu'on ne sait que choisir entre vos trois horreurs,
Et si l'on craindrait moins périr par les terreurs
Des Ténèbres que sous l'Eau sourde, l'Eau profonde,
Ou dans tes bras fardés, Paris, reine du monde!

—Et tu coules toujours, Seine, et, tout en rampant,
Tu traînes dans Paris ton cours de vieux serpent,
De vieux serpent boueux, emportant vers tes havres
Tes cargaisons de bois, de houille et de cadavres!

Leans out, prey to the ill-fated winds of the abyss.
Thought, calm hope, sublime ambition, all these,
Even memory, everything flees, everything vanishes, all of it,
And one is alone with Paris, the Wave and the Night!

—Dire Trinity! Gates of shadow hard as stone!
Mene, Mene, Tekel, Upharsin of dead illusion!
All three of you, o Ghouls of calamity,
Are so terrible that Man, drunk with the misery
Your ghost fingers make piercing his flesh,
Man, an Orestes lacking his Electra,
Under the fatality of your hollow-eyed gaze
Can do nothing and goes straight to the awful precipice;
And you are also all three so keen
To kill and offer wives to the great Worm that one
Doesn't know how to choose between your three horrors,
And whether one would fear less dying by the terrors
Of Darkness than the deep Water, muffled beneath,
Or in your painted arms, Paris, queen of the Earth!

—And you flow, Seine, and while crawling you always
Drag through Paris your ancient serpent's course,
That of the ancient muddy serpent, bearing on
Your cargo of wood, coal and corpses toward your haven!

Marco

Quand Marco passait, tous les jeunes hommes
Se penchaient pour voir ses yeux, des Sodomes
Où les feux d'Amour brûlaient sans pitié
Ta pauvre cahute, ô froide Amitié;
Tout autour dansaient des parfums mystiques
Où l'âme, en pleurant, s'anéantissait.
Sur ses cheveux roux un charme glissait;
Sa robe rendait d'étranges musiques
    Quand Marco passait.

Quand Marco chantait, ses mains, sur l'ivoire,
Évoquaient souvent la profondeur noire
Des airs primitifs que nul n'a redits,
Et sa voix montait dans les paradis
De la symphonie immense des rêves,
Et l'enthousiasme alors transportait
Vers des cieux *connus* quiconque écoutait
Ce timbre d'argent qui vibrait sans trèves,
    Quand Marco chantait.

Quand Marco pleurait, ses terribles larmes
Défiaient l'éclat des plus belles armes;
Ses lèvres de sang fonçaient leur carmin
Et son désespoir n'avait rien d'humain;
Pareil au foyer que l'huile exaspère,
Son courroux croissait, rouge, et l'on aurait
Dit d'une lionne à l'âpre forêt
Communiquant sa terrible colère,
    Quand Marco pleurait.

Marco

When Marco went by, all of the young men would lean
Forward to see the Sodoms of her eyes burn,
The fires of Love consuming without pity
Your poor hovel, o cold Amity;
All around, mystical fragrances would flicker
In which the soul would annihilate itself and cry.
Across her auburn hair a spell would play;
Her dress made a strange music
    When Marco went by.

When Marco sang, her hands on the ivory
Often called forth the black profundity
Of primitive songs that no one has sung since,
And her voice would ascend into the heavens
Of the immense symphony of dream,
Rapture then transporting
Toward *known* heavens whoever was listening
To its ceaseless thrill, its silver timbre,
    When Marco sang.

When Marco cried, her tears were so terrible
They would challenge the most beautiful weapons' sparkle.
Her lips of blood would deepen their crimson
And her despair had about it nothing human;
Like oil on a hearth-fire,
Her rage would swell, red, and one would have heard
A lioness roaring to a bitter wood
Passing on her terrible anger,
    When Marco cried.

. . .

Quand Marco dansait, sa jupe moirée
Allait et venait comme une marée,
Et, tel qu'un bambou flexible, son flanc
Se tordait, faisant saillir son sein blanc;
Un éclair partait. Sa jambe de marbre,
Emphatiquement cynique, haussait
Ses mates splendeurs, et cela faisait
Le bruit du vent de la nuit dans un arbre,
    Quand Marco dansait.

Quand Marco dormait, oh! quels parfums d'ambre
Et de chair mêlés opprimaient la chambre!
Sous les draps la ligne exquise du dos
Ondulait, et dans l'ombre des rideaux
L'haleine montait, rhythmique et légère;
Un sommeil heureux et calme fermait
Ses yeux, et ce doux mystère charmait
Les vagues objets parmi l'étagère,
    Quand Marco dormait.

. . .

. . .

When Marco danced, her skirt of watered
Silk would come and go like the tide,
And like a length of flexible bamboo,
Her flank would twist, making her white breast jut too;
A light launched. Her marble leg, emphatically
Cynical, would hoist
Its dull splendors, and that caused
The sound of the night wind in a tree,
    When Marco danced.

When Marco slept, oh! such fragrances of amber
Mingled with those of flesh would oppress the chamber!
Under the sheets, her back's exquisite line
Would ripple, and in the shadow of the curtains
Her breath ascended, light and rhythmic;
A happy and calm slumber shut
Her eyes, this sweet mystery to enchant
The vague shapes of shelved knick-knacks,
    When Marco slept.

. . .

Mais quand elle aimait, des flots de luxure
Débordaient, ainsi que d'une blessure
Sort un sang vermeil qui fume et qui bout,
De ce corps cruel que son crime absout:
Le torrent rompait les digues de l'âme,
Noyait la pensée, et bouleversait
Tout sur son passage, et rebondissait
Souple et dévorant comme de la flamme,
    Et puis se glaçait.

But when she loved, the waves of lust would
Overflow, as vermilion blood
Does from a wound and smokes and boils from
A cruel body absolved by its own crime:
The torrent would break the dikes of the soul,
Drown thought, everything turned
Upside down in its way, and rebound
Like a flame devouring and supple,
    And then run cold.

César Borgia

Portrait en pied

Sur fond sombre noyant un riche vestibule
Où le buste d'Horace et celui de Tibulle
Lointain et de profil rêvent en marbre blanc,
La main gauche au poignard et la main droite au flanc,
Tandis qu'un rire doux redresse la moustache,
Le duc CÉSAR, en grand costume, se détache.
Les yeux noirs, les cheveux noirs et le velours noir
Vont contrastant, parmi l'or somptueux d'un soir,
Avec la pâleur mate et belle du visage
Vu de trois quarts et très ombré, suivant l'usage
Des Espagnols ainsi que des Vénitiens,
Dans les portraits de rois et de patriciens.
Le nez palpite, fin et droit. La bouche, rouge,
Est mince, et l'on dirait que la tenture bouge
Au souffle véhément qui doit s'en exhaler.
Et le regard, errant avec laisser-aller,
Devant lui, comme il sied aux anciennes peintures,
Fourmille de pensers énormes d'aventures.
Et le front, large et pur, sillonné d'un grand pli,
Sans doute de projets formidables rempli,
Médite sous la toque où frissonne une plume
S'élançant hors d'un noeud de rubis qui s'allume.

Cesare Borgia

Full-Length Portrait

Against the dark background flooding a wealthy hall
Where the bust of Horace and that of Tibullus
Dream in white marble seen in profile from a distance,
Right hand at his side while his left hand's
On his dagger, his moustache turning up with gentle laughter,
He stands out in fancy dress, Duke CESARE.
Black eyes, black hair, black velvet are contrasting,
Amid the opulent gold of an evening,
With the matte beautiful pallor of the face
Heavily shadowed and seen in three-quarters
According to the custom of the Spaniards and the Venetians,
In portraits of kings and patricians.
The nose quivers, thin and straight. The mouth, red,
Is thin, and one would say the drapes are stirred
With the sharp breath that it must exhale.
And that gaze, ranging casual
Ahead of him, as is appropriate to old pictures,
Swarms with great thoughts of adventures
And the brow with a deep furrow, broad and flawless,
Filled with tremendous plans, doubtless,
Ponders them beneath a hat in which a plume shivers
Soaring up from a blazing knot of rubies.

La mort de Philippe II

À Louis-Xavier de Ricard

Le coucher d'un soleil de septembre ensanglante
La plaine morne et l'âpre arête des sierras
Et de la brume au loin l'installation lente.

Le Guadarrama pousse entre les sables ras
Son flot hâtif qui va réfléchissant par places
Quelques oliviers nains tordant leurs maigres bras.

Le grand vol anguleux des éperviers rapaces
Raye à l'ouest le ciel mat et rouge qui brunit,
Et leur cri rauque grince à travers les espaces.

Despotique, et dressant au-devant du zénith
L'entassement brutal de ses tours octogones,
L'Escurial étend son orgueil de granit.

Les murs carrés, percés de vitraux monotones,
Montent droits, blancs et nus, sans autres ornements
Que quelques grils sculptés qu'alternent des couronnes.

Avec des bruits pareils aux rudes hurlements
D'un ours que des bergers navrent de coups de pioches
Et dont l'écho redit les râles alarmants,

Torrent de cris roulant ses ondes sur les roches,
Et puis s'évaporant en de murmures longs,
Sinistrement dans l'air du soir tintent les cloches.

.   .   .

The Death of Philip II

To Louis-Xavier de Ricard

A September sunset bloodies the gloomy plain
and the harsh ridge of the sierras
and the distant fog slowly settling down.

Among low sands the Guadarrama carries
its hurried flood, reflecting here and there a few dwarf olives,
twisting their skinny branches, as it goes.

A large angular rapacious cast of
Sparrowhawks scores the darkening dull red western sky,
Their raucous cry grating through space as they move.

Raising up against the zenith despotically
The brutal pile of its towers' octagons,
The Escorial extends its granite pride. Pierced by

Monotonous windows, square walls of stone
Rise, steep, white, bare, without other
Ornament than sculpted gridirons alternating with crowns.

With noises like the wild roaring of a bear
Wounded by shepherds with blows of a mattock,
Of which the echo repeats the alarming groans, or

A torrent of cries to roll its waves down the rock
And then in long murmurs to evaporate,
The bells ring ominously through the air of dusk.

. . .

Par les cours du palais, où l'ombre met ses plombs,
Circule—tortueux serpent hiératique—
Une procession de moines aux frocs blonds

Qui marchent un par un, suivant l'ordre ascétique,
Et qui, pieds nus, la corde aux reins, un cierge en main,
Ululent d'une voix formidable un cantique.

—Qui donc ici se meurt? Pour qui sur le chemin
Cette paille épandue et ces croix long-voilées
Selon le rituel catholique romain?—

La chambre est haute, vaste et sombre. Niellées,
Les portes d'acajou massif tournent sans bruit,
Leurs serrures étant, comme leurs gonds, huilées.

Une vague rougeur plus triste que la nuit
Filtre à rais indécis par les plis des tentures
À travers les vitraux où le couchant reluit,

Et fait papilloter sur les architectures,
À l'angle des objets, dans l'ombre du plafond,
Ce halo singulier qu'ont voit dans les peintures.

Parmi le clair-obscur transparent et profond
S'agitent effarés des hommes et des femmes
À pas furtifs, ainsi que les hyènes font.

.   .   .

Through palace courtyards shadow has sealed tight,
there winds—a serpent tortuous and hieratic—
a procession of monks in cowls of white

who walk one by one in their ascetic
order, who, barefoot, rope-waisted, taper in hand,
in a fearsome voice wail a canticle.

—Who is dying here? For whom is the straw spread
on the road, for whom are the crosses,
according to Roman Catholic ritual, veiled?—

The room is high-ceilinged, vast and dark. The doors,
black-enamelled, massive mahogany, turn
on hinges that like the oiled locks are soundless.

Sadder than night, a faint ruddiness filters in
Doubtful rays through folds of the wall-hangings,
Through stained glass windows where the setting sun

Gleams, and makes flicker on corbels, in the angle of things,
And in the ceiling's shadow,
The strange halo that one sees in paintings.

Amid the deep transparent chiaroscuro,
Nervous men and women are
Bustling about with furtive steps, the way hyenas go.

. . .

Riches, les vêtements des seigneurs et des dames
Velours, panne, satin soie, hermine et brocart,
Chantent l'ode du luxe en chatoyantes gammes,

Et, trouant par éclairs distancés avec art
L'opaque demi-jour, les cuirasses de cuivre
Des gardes alignés scintillent de trois quart.

Un homme en robe noire, à visage de guivre,
Se penche, en caressant de la main ses fémurs,
Sur un lit, comme l'on se penche sur un livre.

Des rideaux de drap d'or roides comme des murs
Tombent d'un dais de bois d'ébène en droite ligne,
Dardant à temps égaux l'oeil des diamants durs.

Dans le lit, un vieillard d'une maigreur insigne
Égrène un chapelet, qu'il baise par moment,
Entre ses doigts crochus comme des brins de vigne.

Ses lèvres font ce sourd et long marmottement,
Dernier signe de vie et premier d'agonie,
—Et son haleine pue épouvantablement.

Dans sa barbe couleur d'amarante ternie,
Parmi ses cheveux blancs où luisent des tons roux
Sous son linge bordé de dentelle jaunie,

. . .

Sumptuous, the lords' and ladies' garments, velour,
Plush, satin, silk, brocade, ermine,
Singing the ode of luxury in scales of shimmer,

And, piercing the opaque half-light in
Artful distanced flashes, the guards' copper cuirasses
Shoot squibs, aligned and seen three-quarters on.

A man in a black robe with a wyvern's face
(He might as well be studying a book) bends
Over a bed, while caressing his thighs.

Drapes of cloth-of-gold rigid as if masoned
Drop in straight lines from a dais of ebony,
Giving way to the sparkling eye of hard diamonds.

In the bed an old man, notably scrawny,
Between his fingers crooked like stocks of the vine,
Kissing it from time to time, holds a rosary.

His lips make a dull long muttering, last sign
Of life and first sign of the agony of death
—and his breath stinks like an abomination.

In his beard, the color of tarnished amaranth,
In his white hair where reddish tones still glow,
Under his linens edged with

.   .   .

Avides, empressés, fourmillants, et jaloux
De pomper tout le sang malsain du mourant fauve,
En bataillons serrés vont et viennent les poux.

C'est le Roi, ce mourant qu'assisté un mire chauve,
Le Roi Philippe Deux d'Espagne,—Saluez!
Et l'aigle autrichien s'effare dans l'alcôve,

Et de grands écussons, aux murailles cloués,
Brillent, et maints drapeaux où l'oiseau noir s'étale
Pendent deçà delà, vaguement remués!...

—La porte s'ouvre. Un flot de lumière brutale
Jaillit soudain, déferle et bientôt s'établit
Par l'ampleur de la chambre en nappe horizontale:

Porteurs de torches, roux, et que l'extase emplit,
Entrent dix capucins qui restent en prière:
Un d'entre eux se détache et marche droit au lit.

Il est grand, jeune et maigre, et son pas est de pierre,
Et les élancements farouches de la Foi
Rayonnent à travers les cils de sa paupière;

Son pied ferme et pesant et lourd, comme la Loi,
Sonne sur les tapis, régulier, emphatique;
Les yeux baissés en terre, il marche droit au Roi.

.   .   .

Yellowed lace, avid, assiduous, swarming and eager to
Suck out all of the tawny dying man's tainted blood,
In close battalions the lice come and go.

It is the King, dying, helped by an apothecary who is bald,
King Philip the Second of Spain,—Bow to him!
In the alcove the Austrian eagle is rampant, and

Nailed to the walls, the great escutcheons gleam,
And hanging down here and there, stirred a little,
Are many flags, the black bird spreadeagled on them! . . .

—The door opens. Light in a brutal
Flood spurts forth, sweeps along and is soon established
Throughout the room in horizontal

Layers: filled with ecstasy, torchbearers made red,
Ten Capuchins come in and remain in prayer:
One of them breaks free and walks right up to the bed.

He is tall, young and spare,
His tread of stone, and Faith's fierce dartings
Through his eyelashes glare;

His step, firm and slow and heavy like the Law, is sounding
On the carpet, steady, emphatic;
His glance abased, he walks straight to the King.

.   .   .

Et tous sur son trajet dans un geste extatique
S'agenouillent, frappant trois fois du poing leur sein,
Car il porte avec lui le sacré Viatique.

Du lit s'écarte avec respect le matassin,
Le médecin du corps, en pareille occurrence,
Devant céder la place, Ame, à ton médecin.

La figure du Roi, qu'étire la souffrance,
À l'approche du fray se rassérène un peu.
Tant la religion est grosse d'espérance!

Le moine, cette fois, ouvrant son oeil de feu,
Tout brillant de pardons mêlés à des reproches,
S'arrête, messager des justices de Dieu.

—Sinistrement dans l'air du soir tintent les cloches.

◆ ◆ ◆

Et la Confession commence. Sur le flanc
Se retournant, le roi, d'un ton sourd, bas et grêle,
Parle de feux, de juifs, de bûchers et de sang.

— «Vous repentiriez-vous par hasard de ce zèle?
Brûler des juifs, mais c'est une dilection!
Vous fûtes, ce faisant, orthodoxe et fidèle.» —

• • •

And all in his way kneel in an ecstatic
Motion, beating the breast three times with the fist, for
He carries with him the sacred viaticum.

He turns from the bed, deferential assassin or
Buffoon, the body's doctor, on such an occasion, Soul,
Forced to yield to your doctor.

The King's face, drawn with suffering, still
At the friar's approach, so much is religion fat with hope,
Recovers its serenity a little!

This time as the monk opens
His fiery eye, bright with mingled pardons and rebukes,
Messenger of God's law, he stops.

—The bells ring ominously through the air of dusk.

    ◆ ◆ ◆

And the Confession begins. Turning on his side,
The King, in a voice low, subdued and feeble,
Speaks of fire, of Jews, of the stake and blood.

—"You would not by chance regret this zeal?
But it is an act of love toward God to make the Jews burn!
By doing this you were orthodox and faithful."—

    • • •

Et, se pétrifiant dans l'exaltation,
Le Révérend, les bras croisés en croix, tête dressée,
Semble l'esprit sculpté de l'Inquisition.

Ayant repris haleine, et d'une voix cassée,
Péniblement, et comme arrachant par lambeaux
Un remords douloureux du fond de sa pensée,

Le Roi, dont la lueur tragique des flambeaux
Éclaire le visage osseux et le front blême,
Prononce ces mots: Flandre, Albe, morts, sacs, tombeaux.

—«Les Flamands, révoltés contre l'Église même,
Furent très justement punis, à votre los,
Et je m'étonne, ô Roi, de ce doute suprême.

«Poursuivez.»—Et le roi parla de don Carlos.
Et deux larmes coulaient tremblantes sur sa joue
Palpitante et collée affreusement à l'os.

—«Vous déplorez cet acte, et moi je vous en loue.
L'Infant, certes, était coupable au dernier point,
Ayant voulu tirer l'Espagne dans la boue

«De l'hérésie anglaise, et de plus n'ayant point
Frémi de conspirer—ô ruses abhorrées!—
Et contre un Père, et contre un Maître, et contre un Oint!»—

.   .   .

And, freezing in his exaltation,
The Reverend One, his head raised, his arms folded in a cross,
Seems the sculpted spirit of the Inquisition.

Having regained his breath, and in a broken voice,
Laboriously, as if from the bottom of his thought
Tearing out strips of a painful remorse,

The King, whom the tragic glimmerings of torches illuminate,
A bony face and a sallow forehead,
Flanders, Alba, deaths, pillage, tombs, gets five words out.

—"To your credit, the Flemish, who revolted
Against even the Church, were punished most justly,
And at this supreme doubt, o King, I am astonished.

Continue." The King spoke of Don Carlos, and while he
Did, two tears rolled trembling down his cheek,
That quivered and stuck to the bone frightfully.

—"I praise you for it, though you lament this act.
The Infante, certainly, was guilty down to the ground,
Trying to draw Spain into the muck

of English heresy, and furthermore not having hesitated
To conspire—o most detested trickery!—
And against a Father, against a Master, against the Anointed!"

. . .

Le moine ensuite dit les formules sacrées
Par quoi tous nos péchés nous sont remis, et puis,
Prenant l'Hostie avec ses deux mains timorées,

Sur la langue du Roi la déposa. Tous bruits
Se sont tus, et la Cour, pliant dans la détresse,
Pria, muette et pâle, et nul n'a su depuis

Si sa prière fut sincère ou bien traîtresse.
—Qui dira les pensers obscurs que protégea
Ce silence, brouillard complice qui se dresse?—

Ayant communié, le Roi se replongea
Dans l'ampleur des coussins, et la béatitude
De l'Absolution reçue ouvrant déjà

L'oeil de son âme au jour clair de la certitude,
Épanouit ses traits en un sourire exquis
Qui tenait de la fièvre et de la quiétude.

Et tandis qu'alentour ducs, comtes et marquis,
Pleins d'angoisses, fichaient leurs yeux sous la courtine,
L'âme du Roi montait aux cieux conquis.

Puis le râle des morts hurla dans la poitrine
De l'auguste malade avec des sursauts fous:
Tel l'ouragan passe à travers une ruine.

. . .

And then the monk recited the sacred formulae
By which all our sins are forgiven,
And then taking the Host between his two hands fearfully,

He placed it on the King's tongue, all noise having gone
Silent, and the Court, pliant in its distress,
Prayed, mute and pale, and since then no one has known

Whether its prayer was sincere or traitorous
—Who will tell what obscure thoughts the silence
Concealed, complicit mist that rises?—

The King sank back into the ample cushions,
Having received Communion, and already
The bliss of received Absolution was

Opening the eye of his soul to the bright day of certainty,
His features bloomed in an exquisite smile
That had in it both fever and tranquility.

And while dukes, counts and marquises all
Around slipped fearful glances under the curtain,
It rose into conquered heavens, the King's soul.

And in the chest of the noble patient then
With its mad leaps the death rattle howled:
Just as the tempest passes through a ruin.

.   .   .

Et puis, plus rien; et puis, sortant par mille trous,
Ainsi que des serpents frileux de leur repaire,
Sur le corps froid les vers se mêlèrent aux poux.

—Philippe Deux était à la droite du Père.

And then nothing more; and then worms crawled
From a thousand holes like snakes cautious from their lair,
And with the lice on the cold body mingled.

—Philip the Second was at the right hand of the Father.

Épilogue / **Epilogue**

I

Le soleil, moins ardent, luit clair au ciel moins dense.
Balancés par un vent automnal et berceur,
Les rosiers du jardin s'inclinent en cadence.
L'atmosphère ambiante a des baisers de soeur,

La Nature a quitté pour cette fois son trône
De splendeur, d'ironie et de sérénité:
Clémente, elle descend, par l'ampleur de l'air jaune,
Vers l'homme, son sujet pervers et révolté.

Du pan de son manteau que l'abîme constelle,
Elle daigne essuyer les moiteurs de nos fronts,
Et son âme éternelle et sa forme immortelle
Donnent calme et vigueur à nos coeurs mous et prompts.

Le frais balancement des ramures chenues,
L'horizon élargi plein de vagues chansons,
Tout, jusqu'au vol joyeux des oiseaux et des nues,
Tout aujourd'hui console et délivre.—Pensons.

II

Donc, c'en est fait. Ce livre est clos. Chères Idées
Qui rayiez mon ciel gris de vos ailes de feu
Dont le vent caressait mes tempes obsédées,
Vous pouvez revoler devers l'Infini bleu!

.   .   .

I

The sun, less fierce, shines bright in a thinner sky.
Rocked by a lulling autumn breeze,
The garden rosebushes bend rhythmically.
The air around is full of a sister's kisses.

For the time being, Nature has left her throne
Of irony, serenity and splendor:
Toward her perverse, rebellious subject, man,
She descends mild through the fullness of yellow air.

With the hem of her cloak spotted by the abyss,
She deigns to wipe the sweat from our brow,
And her immortal form, her soul's eternities,
Give our slack hasty hearts calm and strength too.

The ancient branches, their cool swaying,
The widened horizon full of indistinct
Song, even the joyous flights of birds and clouds, everything
Today consoles and sets free.—Let us think.

II

Well, it's done. This book is closed. Beloved ideas
That used to score, with your wings of fire, my gray sky,
The backwash from which gave my haunted brow caresses,
You can fly once more toward blue Infinity!

.   .   .

Et toi, Vers qui tintais, et toi, Rime sonore,
Et vous, Rythmes chanteurs, et vous, délicieux
Ressouvenirs, et vous, Rêves, et vous encore,
Images qu'évoquaient mes désirs anxieux,

Il faut nous séparer. Jusqu'aux jours plus propices
Où nous réunira l'Art, notre maître, adieu,
Adieu, doux compagnons, adieu, charmants complices!
Vous pouvez revoler devers l'Infini bleu.

Aussi bien, nous avons fourni notre carrière
Et le jeune étalon de notre bon plaisir,
Tout affolé qu'il est de sa course première,
A besoin d'un peu d'ombre et de quelque loisir.

—Car toujours nous t'avons fixée, ô Poésie,
Notre astre unique et notre unique passion,
T'ayant seule pour guide et compagne choisie,
Mère, et nous méfiant de l'Inspiration.

III
Ah! l'Inspiration superbe et souveraine,
L'Égérie aux regards lumineux et profonds,
Le Genium commode et l'Erato soudaine,
L'Ange des vieux tableaux avec des ors au fond,

.   .   .

And you, Lines that rang out, and you, sonorous Rhyme,
And you, singing Rhythm, and you, delightful Memories,
And you, Dreams, and you, one more time,
Images evoked by my anxious desires,

We must part. Until luckier days
When Art our master will reunite us, goodbye,
Goodbye, sweet companions, charming accomplices!
You can fly once more toward blue Infinity.

Anyway, we've run our course,
And the young stallion of our pleasure, mad
As he is with having run his first race,
Now needs a little rest and a bit of shade.

—For always we have you before us, o Poetry,
Our only star, our only true passion,
Having you only for guide and chosen company,
Mother, distrusting as we do Inspiration.

III
Inspiration superb and sovereign, ah!
Egeria of the luminous deep glance,
Effortless Genius, sudden Erato,
Angel of the old pictures on golden grounds,

. . .

La Muse, dont la voix est puissante sans doute,
Puisqu'elle fait d'un coup dans les premiers cerveaux,
Comme ces pissenlits dont s'émaille la route,
Pousser tout un jardin de poèmes nouveaux,

La Colombe, le Saint-Esprit, le saint Délire,
Les Troubles opportuns, les Transports complaisants,
Gabriel et son luth, Apollon et sa lyre,
Ah! l'Inspiration, on l'invoque à seize ans!

Ce qu'il nous faut à nous, les Suprêmes Poètes
Qui vénérons les Dieux et qui n'y croyons pas,
À nous dont nul rayon n'auréola les têtes,
Dont nulle Béatrix n'a dirigé les pas,

À nous qui ciselons les mots comme des coupes
Et qui faisons des vers émus très froidement,
À nous qu'on ne voit point les soirs aller par groupes
Harmonieux au bord des *lacs* et nous pâmant,

Ce qu'il nous faut, à nous, c'est, aux lueurs des lampes,
La science conquise et le sommeil dompté,
C'est le front dans les mains du vieux Faust des estampes,
C'est l'Obstination et c'est la Volonté!

C'est la Volonté sainte, absolue, éternelle,
Cramponnée au projet comme un noble condor
Aux flancs fumants de peur d'un buffle, et d'un coup d'aile
Emportant son trophée à travers les cieux d'or!

Muse, whose voice is powerful doubtless,
Since in young minds she suddenly
Pushed up a whole garden of new poems, as
These dandelions now spangle the roadway,

Columba, Holy Spirit, Saint Delirium,
Willing Raptures, auspicious Turmoil, ah!
Gabriel and his lute, Apollo and his lyre,
Inspiration, at sixteen I called to you!

What we need, Supreme Poets, for us
Who revere and believe in none of the Gods,
Around whose heads has shone no crown of rays,
Whose steps no Beatrice has ever guided,

For us who chisel our words stroke by stroke
Like goblets and who write moving verse coldly,
For us one never sees strolling in groups by the *lake*
In the evening, harmoniously, rapturously,

What we need, for us, is, by the glimmering
Of lamps, science conquered and sleep held in thrall,
It is the head-in-the-hands of the old Faust in engravings,
It is Stubbornness and it is Will!

It is Will sacred, eternal, absolute,
Stapled to the design as a noble condor is to a buffalo's
Flanks smoking with fear, and by a single wingbeat
Carrying its trophy across golden skies!

. . .

Ce qu'il nous faut, à nous, c'est l'étude sans trêve,
C'est l'effort inouï, le combat non pareil,
C'est la nuit, l'âpre nuit du travail, d'où se lève
Lentement, lentement, l'Oeuvre, ainsi qu'un soleil!

Libre à nos Inspirés, coeurs qu'une oeillade enflame,
D'abandonner leur être aux vents comme un bouleau:
Pauvres gens! l'Art n'est pas d'éparpiller son âme:
Est-elle en marbre, ou non, la Vénus de Milo?

Nous donc, sculptons avec le ciseau des Pensées
Le bloc vierge du Beau, Paros immaculé,
Et faisons-en surgir sous nos mains empressées
Quelque pure statue au péplos étoilé,

Afin qu'un jour, frappant de rayons gris et roses
Le chef-d'oeuvre serein, comme un nouveau Memnon
L'Aube-Postérité, fille des Temps moroses,
Fasse dans l'air futur retentir notre nom!

· · ·

What we need, for us, is boundless study
Unheard-of effort, incomparable battle,
It is night, the bitter night from which rises slowly,
Slowly, the Work, like a sun, out of travail!

Those inspired by Art, hearts a glance can kindle,
Are free to abandon themselves like a birch the wind will blow:
Poor people! Art is not a dissipation of the soul:
Is she of marble, or not, the Venus de Milo?

So we carve with the chisel of our Thought
The untouched block of Beauty, Parian,
And cause beneath our willing hands to rise, immaculate,
Some pure statue in a starry gown,

So that one day, in beams of slate and rose,
Posterity's Dawn, daughter of sad Time,
Might touch it like a new Memnon, the serene masterpiece,
And make resound through the future air our name!

Notes

"The ancient Sages . . . " (p. 2)
Baudelaire (1866) had referred to *Les fleurs du mal* as "un livre satur-
nien" ("a saturnine book"; Le Dantec/Borel, 1074).

"Prologue" (p. 5)
In the 1890 comments written upon the reissue of his first book,
Verlaine speaks of the "epic or didactic tone" of this poem and relates
it to Victor Hugo ("a second-hand Homer") and Leconte de Lisle
(Le Dantec/Borel, 1072).

"Nevermore" (p. 18)
Verlaine owes the title (shared by a poem later in the book) to Poe's
raven's famous refrain; Baudelaire had published his translation of
Poe's poem in 1853.

"After Three Years" (p. 20)
The nostalgic prettiness of the first part of this poem Verlaine has
from Lamartine (whose poem "Le Lac" Verlaine sneers at in the fifth
stanza of the third section of the "Epilogue" to this book), though the
undercutting effect of the poem's last line is his own. Velleda was a Ger-
man priestess who guided an uprising against Rome under Vespasian
(mentioned by Tacitus) and was a popular figure for garden statues in
nineteenth-century France.

"Wish" (p. 22)
Verlaine uses a Greek-derived word, *oaristys*, which goes all the way
back to the magic girdle of Aphrodite (employed by Hera to beguile
Zeus) in the *Iliad* Book XIV; the word might also be translated as
"link of intimacy" or "pillow-talk."

"Lassitude" (p. 24)
Luis de Góngora y Argote (1561–1627), major Spanish poet.

"Parisian Sketch" (p. 34)
The third stanza in this poem was dropped by Verlaine; I have restored it because I think it is effective. The "flickering eye of the blue jets of gas" has in it some of the spiritual queasiness T. S. Eliot will describe (after Laforgue) in "Rhapsody on a Windy Night" (1917).

"Nightmare" (p. 36)
There are earlier poems with the same title by Hugo and Gautier. The poem is based on a German ballad of 1774 by Gottfried August Bürger known to Verlaine in a French translation. *Ritter* is the German word for "knight."

"Marine" (p. 40)
In this poem, perhaps for the first time in the book, there is audible that close coincidence of disturbed landscape and psychic/emotional dis-ease which are Verlaine's particular province. For this reason, the section called "Sad Landscapes," including poems like "Sunsets," "Mystical Dusk," and the incantatory "Sentimental Stroll," provides not so much ekphrastic tableaux as spiritual profiles.

"Night Effect" (p. 42)
The Pléiade edition shows the later (1894) reading of "un gros de hauts pertuisaniers" ("a main body of halberdiers") in line 12, which I have replaced with the original and numerically idiosyncratic reading.

"Sunsets" (p. 50)
Bercot (165) quotes Verlaine's own writing on Baudelaire (looking back to Poe) on the subject of repetition, speaking of "stubborn returns of phrases that simulate the obsessions of melancholy or monomania" ("retours obstinés de phrases qui simulent les obsessions de la mélancholie ou de l'idée fixe"). Form likewise embodies a psychic content in poems such as "Mystical Dusk" and "Sentimental Stroll." The Pléiade

edition (1079) refers to this poem as the first example in the book of a "poème-chant" ("poem-song").

"Classic Walpurgisnacht" (p. 56)
Goethe's *Faust, Part Two* contains a section entitled "Classic Walpurgisnacht." André Lenôtre (1613–1700) was a royal gardener and contributed to the creation of the park at Versailles; Jean-Antoine Watteau (1684–1721), the French painter; Denis Auguste Marie Raffet (1804–1860), French lithographer and illustrator.

"Autumn Song" (p. 60)
One of Verlaine's best-known poems, it became a code for the French Resistance at the time of the Allied invasion of Normandy in 1944.

"Caprices" (p. 67)
Just as the young Verlaine explores the applications of a visual vocabulary to poetry, so, too, in this first volume, he explores the valences of a musical vocabulary, a "capriccio" in music being "an instrumental piece in free form usually lively in tempo and brilliant in style" (*Merriam-Webster's Collegiate Dictionary*). "Autumn Song" ("Chanson d'Automne") may be the most intensely musical poem in the book. The word "mazurka" figures in the poem "Initium," "Nocturne" in the title of Verlaine's long poetic description of the Seine, and he describes the poem "Marco" as a "ritornello." The repeated lines in "Serenade" serve as a kind of musical refrain.

"Jesuitism" (p. 70)
The title of the poem connotes both hypocrisy and intrigue. "Tradéri" is the refrain of a popular song, as Bercot (176) identifies it; and *De profundis* refers to the line in Psalm 130, "Out of the depths have I cried unto thee, O Lord."

"The Song of the Ingenues" (p. 72)

The fifth stanza refers to three exemplary libertines: the real-life Duc de Richelieu (1696–1788), the Chevalier de Faublas, eponymous hero of a work (1787–1790) by Louvet de Couvray, and a certain Caussade, who is mentioned (though he does not appear) as a lover or suitor of the title character in Victor Hugo's play *Marion Delorme* (1831), about a famous French courtesan.

"A Great Lady" (p. 76)

Ninon de Lenclos (1616–1706), famous for her amours and her inconstancy. Bercot (179–80) identifies "Buridan" as a character in an 1832 play by Alexandre Dumas and Félix Gaillardet who exclaims, "These are great ladies" ("Ce sont de grandes dames").

"Mister Wiseman" (p. 78)

Bercot (180) states that Henry Monnier (1799–1877) in 1830 created the figure of Monsieur Prudhomme, the quintessential bourgeois, vain, conventional, platitudinous and stupid, though the French word "prud'homme" can mean a skillful, honest, or upright man; and in "Monsieur Machin" is audible the French word for "so-and-so," "what's-his-name," "thing," or "gadget."

"Initium" (p. 82)

Meaning (as per the last line) "the start of things."

"Savitri" (p. 84)

The story of the princess who manages so to charm Yama, the Hindu god of death, by her virtue (here a Parnassian virtue, that of the "impassible") that he relinquishes her husband Satyavat, makes an interesting parallel to the Greek myth of Alcestis and Admetus. Surya: the sky-god; Chandra: the moon; Vyasa: author of the *Mahabharata*.

"Sub Urbe" (p. 86)
The title connotes our own word "suburb." Verlaine expressed concern to his friend Edmond Lepelletier that the poem might be read as "personal elegy," given the recent death of his father (Le Dantec/Borel, 1083).

"Serenade" (p. 90)
Like Baudelaire's earlier "Le beau navire" (or, for that matter, Shakespeare's Sonnet 130), Verlaine's poem makes a kind of anti-blazon or lover's catalogue of his mistress's charms. Bercot (184) also identifies a parallel with a poem of Théophile Gautier's.

"A Dahlia" (p. 94)
In Homer, Hera is described as being "ox-eyed."

"Nevermore" (p. 96)
"Fatality" ("fatalité") is to be understood as the Saturnine condition, a kind of cosmic bad luck.

"Il bacio" (p. 98)
"Will" is Shakespeare, familiarly addressed. Bercot (186) identifies Verlaine's title as deriving from the title of a contemporary song.

"In the Woods" (p. 100)
Bercot (187) relates these woods to the forest of symbols in Baudelaire's famous poem "Correspondances."

"Parisian Nocturne" (p. 102)
According to Lepelletier, this is the earliest of Verlaine's youthful works to be included in the book; indeed, Lepelletier says that it was passed to him in manuscript by Verlaine during a class in Latin rhetoric! (Le Dantec/Borel, 1084). Clearly, students don't pass notes in class the way they used to. Once its narrative has slogged through the atlas (beguilingly conflating the Mississippi and the Niagara, it seems), the

poem is not without certain pleasing atmospheric effects. *Mene, Mene, Tekel, Upharsin* refers to the magical words announcing King Belshazzar's doom in the biblical book of Daniel, chapter 5.

"Marco" (p. 110)
Verlaine acknowledges that the rhythm and design of this poem are borrowed from a poem entitled "Reverie" by Jules Tardieu, and the name "Marco" is that of a courtesan in a mid-nineteenth-century drama (Bercot, 189). But for the bland prettiness of Tardieu's Minon, Verlaine has substituted a genuine man-eater.

"Cesare Borgia" (p. 116)
Cesare Borgia (1476–1507), natural son of Pope Alexander VI (Rodrigo Borgia), brother of the famous Lucrezia Borgia, served as the model for Machiavelli's ruthless Renaissance man in *The Prince*. Verlaine may be describing, in his most direct exercise in ekphrasis, a portrait by Raphael in the Borghese Gallery in Rome.

"The Death of Philip II" (p. 118)
Hugo and Schiller had both depicted the singularly unattractive King of Spain (1527–1598), who presided over the Inquisition and admittedly had a lot to answer for. But surely Verlaine's lengthy narrative, in merciless terza rima, establishes some kind of high water mark for pure nastiness. Bercot explains (193) that the dedicatee of Verlaine's poem, founder of the *Review of Moral Progress*, was sentenced to three months in prison in 1864 for offenses against religion.

"Epilogue" (p. 135)
The stanza beginning "Those inspired by Art, hearts that a glance can kindle . . . " seems conflicted between the Parnassian "impassive" and the self-abandon of the true artist. The *ars poetica* described here, according to the editors of the Pléiade edition, was not Verlaine's at the

time of his first book and indeed *never* was; they suspect literary opportunism and even intentional parody (Le Dantec/Borel, 1086). The Colossi of Memnon at Thebes are said to sing when touched by the rays of the sun at dawn, a phenomenon explained (to the satisfaction of some) as the expansion of air in the pores of the stone.

The Lockert Library of Poetry in Translation

George Seferis: Collected Poems (1924–1955), translated, edited, and
    introduced by Edmund Keeley and Philip Sherrard
"The Survivor" and Other Poems, by Tadeusz Różewicz, translated
    and introduced by Magnus J. Krynski and Robert A. Maguire
Sounds, Feelings, Thoughts: Seventy Poems by Wisława Szymborska,
    translated and introduced by Magnus J. Krynski and
    Robert A. Maguire
Brocade River Poems: Selected Works of the Tang Dynasty Courtesan
    Xue Tao, translated and introduced by Jeanne Larsen
A Child Is Not a Knife: Selected Poems of Göran Sonnevi, translated
    and edited by Rika Lesser
George Seferis: Collected Poems, Revised Edition, translated, edited,
    and introduced by Edmund Keeley and Philip Sherrard
C. P. Cavafy: Collected Poems, Revised Edition, translated and
    introduced by Edmund Keeley and Philip Sherrard
    and edited by George Savidis
Selected Poems of Shmuel HaNagid, translated from the Hebrew
    by Peter Cole
The Late Poems of Meng Chiao, translated by David Hinton
Leopardi: Selected Poems, translated by Eamon Grennan
Through Naked Branches: Selected Poems of Tarjei Vesaas, translated
    and edited by Roger Greenwald
The Complete Odes and Satires of Horace, translated with introduction
    and notes by Sidney Alexander
Selected Poems of Solomon Ibn Gabirol, translated by Peter Cole
Puerilities: Erotic Epigrams of the Greek Anthology, translated
    by Daryl Hine
Night Journey, by María Negroni, translated by Anne Twitty
The Poetess Counts to 100 and Bows Out, by Ana Enriqueta Terán,
    translated by Marcel Smith